ISBN 978-1-333-52114-1
PIBN 10514874

For support please visit www.forgottenbooks.com

1 MONTH OF
FREE
READING

at

www.ForgottenBooks.com

By purchasing this book you are eligible for one month membership to ForgottenBooks.com, giving you unlimited access to our entire collection of over 1,000,000 titles via our web site and mobile apps.

To claim your free month visit:

www.forgottenbooks.com/free514874

English
Français
Deutsche
Italiano
Español
Português

www.forgottenbooks.com

Mythology Photography **Fiction**
Fishing Christianity **Art** Cooking
Essays Buddhism Freemasonry
Medicine **Biology** Music **Ancient
Egypt** Evolution Carpentry Physics
Dance Geology **Mathematics** Fitness
Shakespeare **Folklore** Yoga Marketing
Confidence Immortality Biographies
Poetry **Psychology** Witchcraft
Electronics Chemistry History **Law**
Accounting **Philosophy** Anthropology
Alchemy Drama Quantum Mechanics
Atheism Sexual Health **Ancient History**
Entrepreneurship Languages Sport
Paleontology Needlework Islam
Metaphysics Investment Archaeology
Parenting Statistics Criminology
Motivational

CARY MEMORIALS

Arms.—"ARGENTUM," Three white roses on a bend sable.
Crest.— A Swan ppr,
Motto.—" Virtute Excerptæ.

By S. F. CARY.

CINCINNATI.

1874.

40,354

2 7.5, '84

"In the time of the reign of Henry V, a certain Knight-Errant of Aragon having passed through divers countries and performed many feats of Arms, to his high commendation, arrived here in England, where he challenged any man of his rank and quality to make trial of his valor and skill at arms. This challenge Sir Robert Cary accepted, between whom a cruel encounter and doubtful combat was waged in Smithfield, London. But at length this noble champion vanquished the presumptious Aragonois, for which Henry V, restored unto him a good part of his father's lands, which for his loyalty to Richard II he had been deprived by Henry IV, and authorized him to bear the Arms of the Knight of Aragon, which the noble posterity continue to wear unto this day; for according to the laws of heraldry, whoever fairly in the field conquers his adversary may justify the wearing of his arms."—BURKE'S HERALDRY.

An old Silver Pitcher, held as an heir-loom in a branch of the family in the U. S. has the above Coat of Arms engraved upon it.—S.F.C.

" Children's children are the crown of old men, and the glory of children is their father's.   PROV. 17, VI.

DEDICATION.

To each and all of the descendants of

John Cary,

a " *Plymouth Pilgrim*," these memorials are dedicated with an earnest hope that every one will endeavor to transmit the name unstained by crime, from generation to genera- tion ; that as one generation passeth away and another cometh, each may rise to a higher and nobler position than its predecessor, in health, in education, in morals, in purity of character and life, and in making the world better and happier ; that each name may be found written in the book of life, when the places that now know it shall know it no more forever.

S. F. C.

INTRODUCTION.

BURKE uttered a noble sentiment when he said: *"Those only deserve to be remembered by posterity who treasure up a history of their ancestors."*

While most persons will assent to the truth of this proposition and while the desire to be remembered and cherished by future generations is universal, very few pay any attention to their ancestral history, and must expect therefore to be forgotten by posterity. Many desire to know more of their ancestors, who they were, what they were, where they lived, and under what circumstances they passed their probation, who have not the leisure to devote to the necessary research, even if the records and persons were extant to furnish the information.

One generation passeth away and another cometh, and the transition is so gradual and yet so rapid, that very soon no one living will be able to say of any of us now upon the busy stage, "I remember him."

The old family bible on the blank leaves of which the

parents have recorded the dates of their birth and marriage, and the births of their children, passes into the possession of one of the descendants, while all the other members of the family are ignorant of every fact except perhaps the date of their respective births, which is recorded only on the tablets of the memory and this perishes with the possessor.

How very few know when or where their parents were born, and a still smaller number can tell the christian names of their grand-parents! The writer has often met men of wealth, intelligence and position who did not know the date of their own birth! In this country especially, families soon scatter to the four winds ; parents and children, brothers and sisters, lose all trace of each other. The labor and difficulty of gathering up the records of seven or eight generations no one can appreciate until he has undertaken the task. In the early history of New England, the births, marriages and deaths were by law made a matter of record in each town. These town-records have been of essential service in compiling these memorials, and but for them many facts could not have been ascertained, as none living knew them.

Incomplete as are the records of some of the families in these memorials, the author will have the satisfaction of introducing as kindred, those who were not aware of relationship, and of gratifying many by informing them in regard to their ancestral lineage. May he not also hope that through this example, others may be induced to undertake a similar work and thus magnify the importance of preserving family histories.

The writer had transmitted to him fragmentary records of kindred long since departed, and tradition said that he was of pilgrim stock. Leisure hours were devoted to ascertain the connecting links in his ancestral line. In the successful search after his own lineage, he gathered a large amount of material which would interest his collateral kindred. As a matter both of curiosity and pleasure he continued his work, until this printed volume is the result.

There is nothing in the history of the CARY FAMILY, to render it worthy of being preserved in this form, which does not belong in common to other families. Every family should have such printed memorials, and not be satisfied with the brief record made in the family bible, which very rarely is extended beyond two generations. / This volume is not designed for public inspection, but it is printed simply to preserve and perpetuate an accurate record of the descendants of John Cary, arranged in generations and families and to assist kindred near and remote, to trace their connection with the parent stock and with others of the name.

It will be observed that the writer has not attempted to trace the descendants of the female members of the families. When the fact was known, the persons to whom they were respectively married is given, that those who wish to trace their maternal connection to this family, can do so. Blank leaves are provided, to enable those who have the volume to extend their records.

It has been a source of very great pleasure to engraft

the scattered Carys upon the parent stock, and follow the branches through to other branches, until the tender and living twigs of the family tree were reached.

. Some who are known to be descendants of 'the same ancestor are omitted in the memorials, because their point of connection could not be distinctly traced. The writer regrets that so few of those, for whose benefit this volume is printed, were disposed to avail themselves of the opportunity of placing it in the hands of their children. Scarcely enough copies have been ordered to pay the expense of printing. We are assured that while the many are indifferent, a few will greatly value their family record.

It would have given increased interest to the volume, if the author could have given more details, in regard to the occupation, modes of life, peculiar characteristics, religious predilections, education, public services, etc. of the persons named therein. He has esteemed himself fortunate to rescue even the names from oblivion and still more fortunate if he could chronicle the year of birth, marriage and death, the three great events in human existence! Who will say that these mere names and dates are uninteresting? What a day was each of these dates to some circle of loving human hearts like our own! How much of joy or sorrow, of hope or despair is hidden under these significant facts? Each is a memorial, not of death only, but of life ; of a human heart that once lived and loved, a heart that kept its steady pulsations through some certain period of time and then ceased to act and mouldered into dust ; of an individual life that had its joys and sorrows, its cares and its burdens, its afflictions and its hopes, its conflicts and its achievements, its opportunities wasted or improved, and its hour of death. Enough is known of the Cary's to enable us to record that in each generation there have been wise and good men. A large average proportion of them were professors of the christian religion, and possessed of those traits peculiar to the early settlers of New England, modified of course by the factitious circumstances of birth and education.

The physical, intellectual, moral and social characteristics however modified by marriage, occupation, etc., have been remarkably preserved.

As a race they have been physically above the common stature, stout, muscular, dark hair and eyes, short necks, great powers of endurance, great tenacity to life, and living to more than the ordinary age. Their mental constitutions have been characterized by strength rather than by brilliancy, fixedness of purpose, persistency in opinion, habit and pursuit. The larger number have been farmers, very few in any generation have accumulated great wealth, none have been mendicants, and so far as can be ascertained, not one has been convicted of crime !

Our work would have been more complete, if persons whom we have addressed would have taken the trouble to have furnished records of their families, which were within their reach. To all those who have responded to our inquiries and aided us in collecting and arranging the facts, we tender our grateful acknowledgments. We believe that there are very few errors in our records. Mistakes are unavoidable to such an undertaking. If the records of some families are more complete than others, it is because the material was at hand to make them so. Doubtless there are some, who with the assistance of these records, will be able to make their own more complete. For the interest and gratification of their posterity, we hope they will avail themselves of the blank leaves for this purpose, as well as to record future marriages, births and deaths.

. In compiling these records, the author has had no other motive, than to furnish his kindred, near and remote, with their family history. The demand for the volume, is necessarily so limited, that he could have had no mercenary object in printing it. No literary fame can result, as there is no opportunity in such a work, for the display of rhetoric or logic. Any person who would expend the time and money, necessary to collect and arrange the facts, could have done as well.

Finally, these memorials make all of us conscious whatever may have been our ancestry, that our existence here is only temporary, that this world is not to be our permanent abode, that this mortal must put on immortality. Like our fathers we must soon pass away and others will occupy our places in the great drama of life, and they again be succeeded by others in a ceaseless stream.

ENGLISH ANCESTRY.

THE family of CARY in England is one of the oldest, as it has been one of the most illustrious and honored in the kingdom. When our ancestors came to the New World they desired doubtless, not only to sever, but forget the ties of blood and begin for themselves a history. If it comported with our purpose, we could give an extended sketch of the Carys of England, running through many centuries. Those who wish to learn particularly of their English ancestry, can consult " Burke's History of the Landed Gentry of England." In the year 1198, according to Sir William Pole, Adam DeKarry was lord of Castle Karry, or Kari, in the county of Somerset. For centuries the castle has existed only in history, and the village situated in that locality is known as " Castle Cary." As early as the reign of Edward the 1st, the name was spelled, C–A–R–Y. William and John Cary represented the county of Devon in Parliament, in the 36th and 42d of Edward III. John Cary was made a Baron of the Exchequer by Richard 11. Sir Robert Cary his son, succeeded to his honors and estates. A proof of the great prowess in arms, of this gallant Knight, is recorded in the following exploit : " In the beginning of the reign of Henry V, a certain Knight-Errant of Aragon, having passed through divers countries and performed many feats of arms, to his high commendation, arrived here in England, where he challenged any man of his rank and quality to make trial of his valor and skill in arms. This challenge Sir Robert Cary accepted, between whom a cruel encounter and a long and doubtful combat was waged in Smithfield, London. But at length this noble champion vanquished the presumptious Aragonois, for which Henry V restored unto him a good part of his father's lands, which for his loyalty to Richard II, he had been deprived by Henry IV and authorized him to bear the Arms of the Knight of Aragon, which the noble posterity of this gentleman continue to wear to this day ; for according to the laws of heraldry whosoever fairly in the field, conquers his adversary, may justify the wearing of his arms."*

SIR WILLIAM CARY, a grand-son of Sir Robert, fell in the battle of Tewksbury, A. D. 1471, fighting under the banner of Lancaster.

LUCIUS CARY, who was Viscount Falkland, Chancellor of the Exchequer under Charles the I, whose marble statue stands at the entrance of the Parliament House, and who was

*See Coat of Arms on the first page. An old Silver Pitcher in possession of one of the family in the United States, an heir-loom of three centuries has the above Coat of Arms engraven on it.

regarded as the greatest man in England of his day, was of this branch of the family. As a statesman he had opposed the errors of the king with all the boldness and inflexibility of Hampden, but with a grace and moderation of which Hampden was incapable. Though Lord Falkland ardently desired liberty for the subject, he was not prepared to oppose the sovereign, and the gallant and accomplished noble took his stand beside his royal master. Learned, witty, elegant and accomplished he was indignant and disgusted at the evident desire of the popular leaders to deluge the country in blood. From the commencement of the civil war he became very melancholy, losing his usual remarkable vivacity. On the morning of the battle of Newbury, he told his friends that he felt confident he would fall in battle that day. This prediction was verified, Hampden the great leader on the side of Cromwell, and Falkland the most illustrious on the side of the king, both fell in that memorable battle.

SIR WILLIAM CARY, married Mary Boleyn, a sister of Anne, the unhappy consort of Henry the VIII. At "Torr Abbey" is preserved the valuable pedigree drawn up by the Heralds' College at the express order of Queen Anne Boleyn. It begins thus : "This pedigree contains a brief of that most ancient family and surname of the Carys and it shows how the family was connected with the noble houses of Beauford, Spencer, Somerset, Bryan, Fulford, Orchard, Holway, etc.

HENRY CARY, was created by his cousin, Queen Elizabeth, *Baron Hunsdon.* Froude in his history shows that he was thoroughly in her confidence and was trusted with many very important matters. His son, Sir Robert Cary, was selected by Elizabeth, to go to Scotland, to assure James I, that the cruel and violent death of Mary, his mother, was not intended by her. Sir Robert was at the bed-side of Elizabeth when she died, and as soon as she breathed her last, he went with all possible despatch to Scotland and was the first to inform James of her death and of his accession to the throne of England.

Queen Elizabeth sought to form a matrimonial alliance between Sir George Cary, her cousin, and Mary Stuart, "Queen of Scots."

"Red Castle," an Irish Estate in county of Donegal and also "White Castle," were granted to branches of the family. The Carys of Ireland are very numerous and although descended from a common ancestor, they uniformly spell the name C–A–R–E–Y. We have not attempted to give a connected history of the family in Great Britain, our object being simply to furnish a few fragments showing the antiquity and distinction of the name. The family in England is still a noble one and traces back its history through the centuries with pride. While none of the name in America will boast of their noble English blood, all will be glad to learn that their ancestral history has been preserved and that there has been in the old world Carys who were worthy of record in the pages of its history.

CARYS IN THE UNITED STATES.

THE name of CARY or CAREY, is quite a common one in almost every State in the Union.   They are all doubtless descendants of De Karry of the Domesday Book, of William
the Conqueror, whether their more immediate ancestors were
of English, Irish or Scotch extraction.   The name was spelled
C–A–R–Y in the reign of Edward III.   Most of those who
spell the name *C–a–r–e–y* are of Irish extraction, but this
rule is not universal as persons not remotely connected spell
the name both ways.   Some whose records are found in this
volume, write the name with an *e*, but they do so without
authority, as their progenitor spelled his name C–A–R–Y.

There were four persons all of whom spelled the name
C–A–R–Y, who came to this country at a very early period,
from each of whom a multitude of families have sprung.

I.   JOHN CARY, joined the Plymouth Colony about 1634.
He came from Somersetshire, England, a few miles from Bristol.   To trace out and connect his descendants has been the
sole purpose of the author.   Whenever he has connected any

family with any other ancestor than John he has omitted them. Of John Cary we shall have more to say in another place.

2. JAMES CARY, joined the Massachusetts Colony about 1635 and settled on a farm, at Chelsea, near where Boston is located. It is still known as the " Cary Farm " and some of his descendants still occupy and own small portions of the original tract. He was born in the city of Bristol, England, in the year 1600; and died in 1681. His grave-stones are still standing in Charlestown, Massachusetts and the inscription is still legible.

It is probable that James and John were nearly related, as they emigrated from the same neighborhood in England, but they were probably not brothers. Edward M. Cary, Esq. of Boston, an educated gentleman, a descendant of James Cary, who has given considerable attention to the genealogy of the family, thinks that James and John and Miles were brothers, and this opinion is expressed in Mitchell's History of Bridgewater. We think the *known* facts do not justify this conclusion. Edward M. Cary's tradition is that " In the reign of King James I there were five brothers of the name of Cary in the city of Bristol, England, the last resided for a time in Plymouth, from which place he removed to Charlestown and settled there as a merchant. His christian name was *James*. Jonathen Cary when in England many years ago in search of family records, wrote " when ye quarrells between James and his parliament took place *three* of *five* brothers of ye name of Cary, in ye city of Bristol, adopted a resolution to leave Eng-

land. One of them went to Ireland, two came to America—
one of these James settled in New England, ye other in Virginia." James Cary had four sons and two daughters. One
of the sons, Nathaniel, followed the sea. It is recorded that
he took his wife, Elizabeth, to Salem as a witch. She was
tried and condemned. While in prison with the help of a
daughter, she escaped and took a vessel for Liverpool whither
her husband had already sailed. The first person her husband met on his arrival at Liverpool was his wife. When he
saw her he exclaimed "you must be a witch." She replied
"don't be a fool Nat. like the rest of your countrymen."

Jonathan, another son of James, born in 1646, died in
1737 at the age of 92 years. From this son has descended a
numerous posterity. Richard Cary, aid-de-camp of General
Washington, was his great grand-son. George Cary a wealthy and highly esteemed merchant, (retired,) of Boston,
connected with the family of Robert Treat Paine. William
F. Cary, Esq., of New York City, extensively engaged in the
Tea trade with China; the wives of President Felton and
Prof. Agassiz of Harvard, are of this branch of the Cary
stock. Samuel Cary who graduated in the class of 1731 and
whose life was illustrated by repeated acts of bravery, good
conduct and exact probity, and who died at Chelsea, Mass.,
of wounds received in the French and Indian war, 1755-63
was also of this branch. The old Cary mansion built of oak,
now near 250 years old is still standing and in a perfect state
of preservation. It may stand a century longer unless

destroyed by casualty or the hands of man. We could give a more extended sketch of the descendants of James Cary but it does not comport with our design.

3. COL. MILES CARY, joined the Virginia Colony about 1640. He was the son of John Cary, of Bristol, who was a half-brother of James of the Massachusetts Colony. John the father of Miles, and James of the Massachusetts Colony were sons of William Cary, mayor of the city of Bristol in 1600. According to our tradition then, James of Charlestown, Mass. was a half-uncle of Col. Miles, of Virginia Colony, and that John of Plymouth, was not a brother of either. Miles died at Warwick, Virginia, in 1667. From him have descended some who were distinguished in the early history of Virginia. Col. Archibald Cary, President of the House of Burgesses at the beginning of the Revolutionary War, a contemporary and intimate friend of Patrick Henry, and alike distinguished for their fiery zeal in the cause of independence, was a descendant of Miles. The wife of Frank Blair, Sr. and mother of Hon. Montgomery and Hon. Frank P., are descendants of Col. Archibald Cary. W. M. Cary, Esq. of Baltimore, a gentleman greatly interested and well-informed in the genealogy of the family is a lineal descendant of this revolutionary hero. The greater number of the Carys in the Southern States are descendants of Col. Miles Cary.

4. THOMAS CARY came from Scotland in the year 1680 and settled in the Delaware Colony. His descendants are not so numerous and are widely scattered. Judge John Cary

an ex-member of Congress, living in Wyandotte County, O. is of this line.*

There have been numerous immigrations of Carys to this country from England and Ireland at later periods.

MATTHEV CARY a distinguished Book Publisher of Philadelphia in the early part of this century, came from Ireland. His son and successor Henry C. Cary, of Philadelphia, has a world-wide reputation as a scholar and writer on political economy, social sciences, etc. All our prominent statesmen know him and seek his counsels on the subjects of Tariff and Finance. The Irish Careys universally spell the name C–A–R–E–Y.

Having said this much of the different families of Carys in this country, we shall hereafter only refer to the descendants of John of Plymouth.

*The author has found descendants of Thomas in Delaware, Pennsylvania, Maryland and Ohio.

DESCENDANTS

OF

JOHN CARY.

—

FIRST GENERATION.

No. 1,

JOHN CARY the ancestor and progenitor of the families herein recorded, came from Somersetshire, near the city of Bristol, England, about 1634, and joined the Plymouth Colony. The precise date of his arrival in the New World is not known. It is certain that he did not come over in the "Mayflower," the "Fortune" or the "Ann." There are various traditions in regard to his immediate ancestry and different opinions as to his near relationship to James and Miles Cary, the former settling at Charlestown, Mass. and the latter near Jamestown, Va. The writer has had access to a manuscript more than one-hundred years old and written by a grand-son of John, which says that John Cary when a youth was sent by his father to France to perfect his education, and that while absent his father died. On returning home to Somersetshire he differed with his brothers about the settle-

ment of their father's estate.   He compromised by receiving
£100 as his portion and immediately sailed for America.   As
the writer of the manuscript had better means of knowing the
facts which he recorded than we can know, we adopt his
statement as true.   We find his name among the original proprietors and first settlers of Duxbury and Bridgewater.   His
name occurs in the original grant as well as in the subsequent
deed made by Ousamequin, the sachem or chief of the Poc-
konocket Indians, in A. D. 1639.   This deed was made to
Miles Standish, (Captain of the Mayflower,) Samuel Nash and
Constant Southworth, as Trustees, in behalf of William Bradford, *John Cary*, and fifty-two others therein named. , The
deed embraced fourteen miles square and was designated as
" Satucket." The consideration named in the deed was "*seven
coats, a yard and a half in a coat; nine hatchets; eight hoes;
twenty knives; four moose skins and ten and a half yards of
cotton.*"   Ousamequin was afterwards called "*Massasoit.*"
The fourteen miles square was parcelled out to the fifty-four
persons, each having his share assigned him by lot. John
Cary drew a tract one mile wide, from the north line of the
town, running southward seven miles.   West Bridgewater is
quite level and somewhat marshy, but our ancestor was fortunate enough to get a pretty good farm.   Some of his descendants of the eighth generation still occupy a portion of the
original tract.   Each settler had at first a grant of a "house
lot " of six acres on the town river " Nippenicket."   The first
lots were taken up in West Bridgewater; They were laid out

contiguous, with a view to mutual aid and defense in case of assault by hostile Indians.   Bridgewater was the first interior settlement in the old Plymouth Colony.   "Duxbury New Plantation" was incorporated into a new and distinct town and called Bridgewater, in 1656.   John Cary was elected Constable the first and only officer elected in the town that year.   He was elected the first Town Clerk and held the office each consecutive year until 1681.   In 1656 there were but ten freemen in the town, of which John Cary was one; in May, 1667 seven more freemen were added.   In the same year John Cary was appointed on a jury "to lay out the ways requisite in the town."   In 1667 Deacon Willis and John Cary were chosen "to take in all the charges of the late war, (King Phillip's) since June last and the expenses of the scouts before and since June."

We can know but little of the traits of character of the progenitor of the numerous race, many of whose records we have gathered up.   He was prominent among his fellows and participated actively in town meetings; was intelligent, well-educated and public-spirited.   The tradition is that he taught the first latin class in the colony.   Doubtless he was deeply imbued with puritan principles and a decided christian, as were all the Bridgewater settlers.   In a preface to a sermon (by the first minister, the Rev. Mr. Keith, June 14, 1717) signed by Increase Mather and Cotton Mather, occur the following passages: "The first settlers of Bridgewater, were a set of people who made religion their main interest, and it became their glory." "Remarkable was the fate of Bridgewater, a most praying and a most pious town ; seated in the very midst of the war ; that although they were often assaulted by formidable numbers of the enemies, yet in all their sharp assaults they never lost one of their inhabitants, young or old." The opinion entertained was that their piety shielded them from savage cruelty and outrage. It is an interesting fact that Mr. Keith, their first pastor, who was from Aberdeen, Scotland, was installed in 1663 and preached there 56 years.

JOHN CARY m. Elizabeth, a daughter of Francis Godfrey, one of the first settlers of Bridgewater in 1644. The year of his birth is not known, he died in 1681.

His children were :

   I.   JOHN, b. 1645. No. 2:

  II. FRANCIS, b. 1647. No. 3.

 III. ELIZABETH,* b. 1649.

 IV. JAMES, b. 1652. No. 4.

  V. MARY, b. 1654. d. unm.

 VI. JONATHAN, b. 1656. No. 5.

VII. DAVID, b. 1658. No. 6.

VIII. HANNAH, b. 1661. d. unm.

 IX. JOSEPH, b. 1663. No. 7.

  X. REBECCA.† b. 1665.

 XI. SARAH, b.. 1667. n. t.

*ELIZABETH m. Deacon William Britt, had but one child, Bethiah, who m. Thos. Heywood, of E. Bridgewater in 1706.

†REBECCA m. Samuel Allen, in 1685, and had five children, viz.: Samuel b. 1686, Ephraim 1689, Timothy 1691, Joseph 1693, Mehitabel 1695. From this branch of the family descended Rev. D. Allen, D. D., late of Lane Seminary, and many other distinguished men.

⌒ JOHN CARY, son of John, No. 1, b. 1645, m. Abigail, dau. of Samuel Allen, 1670, lived in Bridgewater until 1680 and then removed to Bristol, R. I., where he resided until his death in July, 1721. His will was admitted to Probate in Bristol, August, 1721 ; the inventory of his property amounted to £700. The will of his wife was recorded in 1729.

John Cary and his wife were buried in the old Cemetery on the common ; his grave-stone of slate is still in good order and the inscription legible.. It reads thus :

"Here lies ye body of Deacon John Cary, a shining pattern of piety, whose spirit returned to God who gave it, July 14, 1721, in ye 76 year of his age."

"A man of prayer so willing to do good,
"His highest worth who of us understood.
"Fear God, love Christ, help souls their work to mend.
"So like this Saint fit for bliss without end."

This stone now stands in the yard the Congregational Church. / /

His children were :

  I. JOHN, b. Nov. 6, 1670. d. Nov. 29, 1671.

  II. SETH, b. January 23, 1672. n. t.

  III. JOHN, b. December 9, 1674. No. 8.

  IV. NATHANIEL, b. Nov. 24, 1676. d. without issue, December 11, 1739.

  V. ELEAZER, b. September 27, 1678. No. 9.

  VI. JAMES, b. June 10, 1680. No. 10.

  VII. BENJAMIN, b. October 27, 1681. No. 11.

  VIII. ELIZABETH, b. May 23, 1683: m. Ephraim Kidder.

  IX. ABIGAIL,* b. August 3, 1684.

  X. JOSIAH, b. May 6, 1686. No. 12.

  XI. TIMOTHY, b. February 16, 1688. n. t.

No. 3.

FRANCIS CARY, son of John, No. 1, b. in Bridgewater, 1648, was named for his maternal grandfather, Francis Godfrey, m. Hannah, dau. of William Britt, 1676, (an original proprietor and prominent citizen,) lived in Bridgewater, where he d. 1718.

*ABIGAIL, m. Samuel Howland, May 6, 1708, and had ten children whose posterity is very numerous and widely scattered. Capt. William Pearse, who died at Bristol, in February, 1867, at the age of 95, was a grand son of Abigail.

His children were:

    I.   SAMUEL, b. 1677. No. 13.

    II.   EPHRAIM, b. 1679. No. 14.

   III. MARY,* b. 1681.

   IV. LYDIA,† b. 1683.

    V. MEHITABEL, b. 1685, m. Joseph Lucas, 1727, no issue.

No. 4.

JAMES CARY, son of John No. 1, b. in Bridgewater, 1652, m. Mary Shaw, of Weymouth, Mass., 1682, settled in Bristol where he died 1706; his wife d. 1736.

His children were:

    I.   MERCY, b. 1686, m. Daniel Thurston, 1713.

    II.   MARY, b. 1689. n. t.

   III. JAMES, b. 1692. No. 15.

   IV. HANNAH, b. 1696. n. t.

    V. ELIZABETH,‡ b. 1700.

*MARY, m. Nicholas Whitman, 1715, had two sons Eleazer b. 1716, and Benjamin b. 1719; Eleazer removed to Abington, Mass. and d. at 90 years old. Mary the mother d. 1719. Judge Whitman, an eminent lawyer and jurist of Cincinnati, O., is of this family.

†LYDIA, m. Joseph Edson, 1704 and had Hannah 1709, Lydia 1711. Joseph 1712, Bethiah 1715, John 1717, Daniel 1720, David 1722, Jesse 1724, James 1726. Lydia the mother d. 1762. She is the maternal ancestor of a number of the Edsons in the United States.

‡ELIZABETH, m. John Whitman, 1728, and had Samuel 1730, Elizabeth 1732, John 1735, James 1739. The mother died 1742.

No. 5.

Jonathan Cary, son of John, No. 1, b. in Bridgewater, 1656, m. Sarah daughter of Samuel Allen, and d. 1695, in Bridgewater.

His children were:

    I.   Recompense, b. about 1688. No. 16.

    II. John, b. about 1690. No. 17.

    III. Jonathan, b. about 1692. No. 18.

No. 6.

David Cary, son of John, No. 1, b. in Bridgewater, 1658; went with his brother John to Bristol, R. I. in 1680; was one of the original proprietors of the town. He was a carpenter by trade and established a brewery, some of the ruins of which still remain. His dwelling stood 100 years. He was a man of education, influence and piety; was chosen deacon of the church in 1683 and held the office until his death in 1718. His estate was inventoried at £811.; a wealthy man at that day. He provides in his will that if his son Henry, shall proceed in learning so far as to enter college, then his son Peter shall pay the charge for his college learning. He m. Elizabeth ———

His children were:

I. ELIZABETH, b. March 7, 1691. m. Daniel Smith.

II. MEHITABLE, ⎫   TVINS   ⎧ m. — Wardwell.

III. BETSHEBA, ⎭ b. Aug. 14, 1693. ⎩ m. — Howland.

IV. SARAH, b. January 21, 1695, d. 1700. ٭

V. BETHIAH, b. January 22, 1697. m. — Goreham.

VI. DAVID, b. February 20, 1699. No. 19.

VII. PETER, b. November 9, 1701. n. t.

VIII. MARY, b. November 6, 1703. d. 1712.

IX. PRISCILLA, b. May 9, 1709. m. Joseph Gladding, 1726.

X. HENRY,* b. June 4, 1711.

No. 7.

JOSEPH CARY, son of John, No. 1, b. in Bridgewater, 1663, when a young man went to Norwich, Connecticut, and became one of the original proprietors of Windham and shortly afterwards bought one-thousand acres of land for £10, 9 shillings, February 9, 1694. He took position with the first men of the town in civil and ecclesiastical affairs; he was chosen repeatedly to serve in the most important offices, civil, military and religious; he was one of the original members of the First Congregational Church in Windham and was chosen at its organization Dec. 10, A. D. 1700, a deacon, and continued to

---

*HENRY graduated at Harvard College, 1733. m. and emigrated to Vermont; had a large family, none of whom I have been able to find. He d. in 1801 at the age of 90 years.

hold the office until his death. So highly was he esteemed that at his death he was buried by his townsmen "*under arms*," at that day, a very unusual occurrence. He was a very large, athletic man, as were the Carys generally. He was twice married; his first wife, Hannah ———, d. 1691, and he m. Mercy, the widow of Jonathan Rudd. He d. January 10, 1722 ; his widow d. 1741, aged 84 years.

His children were :

    I.   JOSEPH, b. May 5, 1689. No. 20

   II.   JABEZ, b. July 12, 1691. No. 21.

  III.   HANNAH,* b. March 4, 1693.

  IV.   JOHN, b. January 23, 1695. No. 22.

    V.   SETH, b. July 29, 1697. No. 23.

  VI.   ELIZABETH,† b. April 17, 1700.

*HANNAH, m. Deacon Nathaniel Skiff, 1716, and had one son, Joseph, d. 1813 aged 95 years. She lived and died in the now Borough of Willimantic, Ct., August 22, 1775, aged 82 years.

†ELIZABETH, m. Seth Palmer, 1720, and d. 1739.

THIRD GENERATION.

No. 8.

JOHN CARY, son of John, No. 2, b. in Bridgewater, December 9, 1674; went with his father when a boy to Bristol, R. I. m. a Miss Arnold, March 13, 1700; lived for a time at Newport, R. I., but d. in Bristol, April 25, 1711.

His children were:

I.   PHEBE, b. March 5, 1701.   n. t.

II.   ABIGAIL, b. November 4, 1702.   n. t.

III.   JOHN, b. November 21, 1704.   n. t.

IV.   DEMARIS, b. October 10, 1706.   m. John Hull, April 23, 1726 and had 14 children and a numerous posterity.

No, 9.

ELEAZER CARY, son of John, No. 2, b. in Bridgewater, September 27, 1678; removed with his father to Bristol, R. I. m. Lydia ——, in 1700, and about 1716 removed to Windham, Ct., where his uncle Joseph (No. 7,) resided.   He bought of Richard Abbe, Esq., ' eighty-six acres of land and meadow" at the end of Cedar Swamp meadow, for £110, January 16, 1717.   This was about one mile east of Windham Center and was called and still retains the name of " *Christian Street,*" from the piety of the early settlers. Three or four generations of this branch of Carys lived in this vicinity.   Eleazer was chosen deacon of the First Church in Windham in 1729, which office he held until his death. He was called Capt. Cary and from his first arrival there took an active part in all public affairs.   From the town records we learn that he was one of the prominent and substantial men.   The Rev. Thomas Clapp, afterwards president of Yale College was at that time pastor of this church in Windham.   From his will dated March 6, 1752, it appears he had eleven children; he d. July 28, 1754, aged 76 years.

1 lis children were :

I.   ELIZABETH,* b. March 25, 1701.

II.   ABIGAIL,† b. January 15, 1703.

III. ANN,‡ b. September 21, 1708.

IV.   LYDIA,|| b. ———, 1710.

V.   ELEAZER, b. November 19, 1713.   No. 24.

VI.   MARY,§ b. March 23, 1716.

VII. MARTHA, b. ———, 1718. d. unm. January 25,
      1774.

VIII. SARAH, b. April 10, 1720. d. May 4, 1726.

IX.   WILLIAM. b. March 4, 1722. d. May 2, 1726.

X.   ALATHEA, b. May 12, 1724. d. February 22, 1737.

XI.   WILLIAM, b. October 28, 1729.   No. 25.

---

*ELIZABETH, m. Joshua Wright, and had a large family, in Windham.

†ABIGAIL, m. Jeremiah Ripley, by whom she had seven children, two
of whom, Eleazer and Lieut. Chas. Ripley, of the Revolutionary war were
prominent men. Lieut. Chas. Ripley died in captivity, with the British
Army. She d. October 16, 1766.

‡ANN, m. Nathan Dennison, April 1, 1736, who commanded a portion
of the troops at Wyoming, Pa., at the time of the memorable massacre, July
1778. She had a large family.

||LYDIA, m. David Ripley, of Windham, Ct. and was the mother of Rev.
Hezekiah Ripley, (see Sprague's Annals, vol. 1, pages 648, 649, 650,) and
Rev. David Ripley, and other talented sons. Gen. William Ripley of the war
of 1812, who d. at Painesville, Ohio, was her grand-son.

§MARY, m. Gideon Bingham, of Windham, and is the ancestress of a
numerous and respectable race. Samuel Bingham, cashier of Windham
Bank, and I believe Hon. John A. Bingham, of Ohio are descendants.

No. 10.

JAMES CARY, son of John, No. 2, b. in Bridgewater, June 10, 1680 ; went with his father to Bristol, R. I.; m. Bridget ————; settled in Newport, R. I.

His children were:

I. REBECCA, b. May 17, 1707, n. t.

II. SETH, b. June 5, 1709. Probably emigrated to the state of New York ; cannot distinctly connect families with him.

No. 11.

BENJAMIN CARY, son of John, No. 2, b. at Bristol, R. I. October 27, 1681 ; was a man of considerable distinction ; was several years town clerk ; succeeded his father as deacon of the church. In the cemetery at Bristol are two upright stones, the inscriptions on which are as follows :

" Here lies interred ye body of Deacon Benjamin Cary, who departed this life January 20, 1734, in ye 54 year of his age." " In memory of Susannah, widow of Deacon Benjamin Cary, died August 10, 1764, aged 77 years."

Mrs. Cary in her will, proven December 4, 1764, gives to her two surviving sons, Benjamin and Nathaniel, all her real estate and to her grand-daughter, Susannah Cary, £100 lawful money; to her daughter, Elizabeth Clark, all her "silver plate and indoor moveables, *also her servant* girl named Caty." The estate of Benjamin was inventoried at £8,800. There is a monument in the old cemetery in memory of six of his children who died of "throat distemper," (our modern diptheria.) Mrs. Cary was bereft of her husband and six children within a period of two years. It is recorded that he died suddenly of something like a sinking chill.

His children were:

I.   BENJAMIN, b. about 1706. No. 26.

II.   ALLEN, b. July, 1708. No. 27.

III. NATHANIEL, b. ——, 1710, d. December 1710.

IV.   NATHANIEL, b. November 2, 1712. No. 28.

V.   BETHIAH, b. February 8, 1716, d. June 7, 1736.

VI.   ABIGAIL, b. February 11, 1718, d. May 10, 1736.

VII. ELIZABETH, b. February 20, 1720, m. Gamaliel Clark, November 17, 1740.

VIII. MEHITABEL, b. September 22, 1722, d. June 4, 1736.

IX.   JOHN, b. September 22, 1725, d. May 29, 1736.

X.   LYDIA, b. ——, 1727, d. May 27, 1736.

XI.   SETH, b. ——, 1729, d. March 10, 1736.

XII. JOSEPH, b. ——, 1730, d. May 10, 1736.

XIII. SUSANNAH, b. ——, 1732, m. Daniel Throop.

XIV. MARY, b. ——, 1734, d. May 9, 1737.

No. 12.

Josiah Cary, son of John, No. 2, b. in Bristol, R. I. May 6, 1686; m. in Bristol to Ruth Reynolds, November 9, 1710; he d. June 26, 1739.

His children were:

    I. Joseph, b. January 10, 1712. n. t.

    II. Nathaniel,* b. February 6, 1714.

*Nathaniel, m. Tabitha Howland, December 11, 1737, and died childless 1740.

No. 13.

Samuel Cary, son of Francis, No. 3, b. in Bridgewater, Mass., 1677; m. Mary Pool, 1704 and removed from the town to Duchess county, N. Y.

His children were:

    I. Joseph,* b. 1705.

    II. Lydia, b. 1706.

    III. Alice, b. 1707.

    IV. Elizabeth, b. 1709.

    V. Samuel,* b. 1711.

    VI. David,* b. 1713.

    VII. Nathan,* b. 1716.

    VIII. Eleazer, b. 1718. No. 29.

*The compiler of these records has found many, who are undoubtedly descendants of these four brothers, but the precise connection he has been unable to trace, although he has spent much time and effort to do so. Some of their descendants are found in Duchess and Albany counties, N. Y. Samuel, Abraham and Nathan who had large families in Albany county, N. Y.; John Cary, who died in Oneida county; Joseph Cary, of Wisconsin; Leonard Cary, of Cohoes, N. Y. and Martin Cary, of Sheridan, N. Y., are believed to be descendants of Joseph. It is believed that Nathan went to Pennsylvania and settled in the Wyoming Valley with Eleazer.

No. 14.

EPHRAIM CARY, son of Francis, No. 3, b. in Bridgewater, Mass., 1679; m. Hannah Waldo, in 1709; lived and died in his native town; d. 1765; his wife d. 1777, aged 90 years.

His children were:

    I.   MEHITABLE, b. 1709, m. Benjamin Allen, and had a large family.

    II. EZRA, b. 1711. No. 30.

    III. ZECHARIAH, b. 1713. No. 31.

    IV. EPHRIAM, b. 1714. No. 32.

    V. DANIEL, b. 1716. No. 33.

No. 15.

JAMES CARY, the only son of James, No. 4, b. in Bridgewater, Mass., 1692; m. Sarah Shaw, 1722; he d. in 1762, and having survived his only son the name became extinct in this line, he being the only son of his father.

His children were:

    I.   SARAH, b. 1723, m. William Barrell, 1741.

    II. JOSHUA, b. 1726, d. unm., 1747.

No. 16.

Deacon Recompence Cary, son of Jonathan, No. 5, b. in Bridgewater, Mass., 1688; m. Mary Crossman, in Bridgewater, 1711, and resided there during his whole life, a man of influence; he d. 1759.

His children were ;

     I. Seth, b. 1714, d. uum., 1742.

    II. Ichabod, b. 1715. No. 34.

   III. Ebenezer, b. 1717, d. unm. 1744.

   IV. Sarah,* b. 1718.

    V. Simeon, b. 1719. No. 35.

   VI. Zebulon, b. 1721. No. 36.

  VII. Jonathan, b. 1723. No. 37.

 VIII. Josiah, b. 1724, d. unm. 1743.

   IX. Mary, b. 1726, m. Joseph Crossman, of Easton.

    X. Abigail, b. 1729. n. t.

No. 17.

John Cary, son of Jonathan, No. 5, b. in Bridgewater, Mass., 1690; lived in Bridgewater, owned a grist mill at "Orrs

*Sarah, m. Benjamin Haywood, 1742, and had a large family; d. 1776·

Works;" he was m. four times; the following distich was common in after times:

> " Experience and Mary, Susannah and Sarah,
>
> These were the wives of old John Cary."

By his first wife he had five children ; by his second, one ; and by his third, two.   He lived to old age.

His children were:

    I.   JOHN, b. 1719.   No. 38.

   II.   MARTHA, b. 1721, m. Daniel Cary, 1742.

  III.   HENRY, b. 1723.   No. 39.

  IV.   SUSANNAH, b. 1725.   n. t.

   V.   BERIAH, b. 1729.   No. 40.

  VI.   MOLLY, b. 1732.   n. t.

 VII.   THANKFUL, b. 1745.   n. t.

VIII.   HULDAH, b. 1750.   n. t.

No. 18.

JONATHAN CARY, son of Jonathan, No. 5, b. in Bridgewater, Mass., 1692; lived in S. Bridgewater ; m. first, Susannah Keith ; she died childless, and he married Experience Carver, ~~1729.~~ *1718* He died 1766, aged 74 years.

His children were :

  I. SETH, b. 1721. n. t.

  II. ELEAZER, b. 1723. No. 41.

  III. SUSANNA,* b. 1725.

  IV. ANNE,† b. 1728.

  V. JONATHAN, b. 1730. No. 42.

  VI. ELIPHALET,‡ b. 1732.

  VII. EXPERIENCE, b. 1734. n. t.

 VIII. BENJAMIN, b. 1738. n. t.

  IX. JESSE, b. 1742. n. t.

No. 19.

DAVID CARY, son of David, No. 6; b. in Bristol, R. I., February 20, 1699; m. first, Rachel Bates of Dorchester, Mass., January 26, 1721 ; and second, Mary Canada, June 9, 1729.

*SUSANNA, m. William Hooper, 1759; d. 1795.

†ANNE, m. Hon. Nathan Mitchell, 1754, and left a numerous family.

‡ELIPHALET was a major in the war of the Revolution ; m. in advanced life to Hannah, widow of Josiah Edson ; had no children and d. over 90 years of age.

His children were:

   I.   DAVID, b. November 23, 1729. Emigrated to Nova Scotia.

  II.   EDVARD, b. May 7, 1732. Settled in Taunton, Mass. n. t.

 III.   MARY, b. August 9, 1733. m. —— Wilbour, no issue.

 IV.   THOMAS, b. January 19, 1735. No. 43.

  V.   NATHAN, b. Feb'y 5, 1737. Went to Vermont. n. t.

 VI.   MICHAEL, b. January 23, 1739. No. 44.

No. 20.

JOSEPH CARY, son of Deacon Joseph, No. 7, b. in Norwich, Ct., May 5, 1689 ; went with his father to Windham, Ct.; m. Abigail Bushnell, July 4, 1711 ; his father gave him a farm in "Scotland Society," a part of Windham, where he died 1722.

His children were:

   I.   ABIGAIL, b. September 7, 1714. m. Elijah Dean, Middletown, Ct.

  II.   JOSEPH, b. December 10, 1715. d. unm.

 III.   ZEROIAH, b. May 22, 1715, d. in Providence, R. I., 1747.

 IV.   HANNAH, b. ——, 1720. n. t.

The Cary name became extinct in this branch of the family.

No. 21.

JABEZ CARY, son of Deacon Joseph, No. 7, b. in Norwich, Ct., July 12, 1691 ; m. Hannah Hendee, November 15, 1722 ; settled first in Windham, afterwards in Preston and finally in Mansfield, Ct., where he d. in 1760.

His children were:

I. JOSEPH, b. September 28, 1723.   No. 45.

II. HANNAH, b. July 6, 1725. d. unm. December 25, 1741.

III. JABEZ, b. July 30, 1727.   No. 46.

IV. NATHANIEL, b. October 23, 1729.   No. 47.

V. EBENEZER, b. ——, 1732.   No. 48.

VI. DAVID, b. ——, 1734.   m. Mary Webber, 1756, in Mansfield, Ct.   n. t.

VII. MARY, b. Nov. 17, 1739.   m. Benjamin Crosby, of Mansfield, Ct.

VIII. BENJAMIN, b. January 25, 1741.   d. in infancy.

No. 22.

JOHN CARY, son of Deacon Joseph, No. 7, b. in Windham, Ct., June 23, 1695 ; m. Hannah Thurston, May 15, 1716 ; his father gave him 100 acres of land in "Scotland Society," (a part of Windham,) east of Merrick Brook ; he and his wife were original members of the Third Church in Windham, organized 1735 ; he was a prominent and influential citizen ; his wife was from Bristol, R. I., and a sister of

Mehitabel Thurston, wife of Nathaniel Huntington and mother of Governor Samuel Huntington, one of the signers of the Declaration of Independence.

John Cary d. January 11, 1776, aged 81 years ; his widow d. 1780, aged 86 years. His personal estate amounted to £397.

His children were:

    I.   JOHN, b. April 12, 1717, No. 49.

    II. BENEIJAH, b. March 7, 1719. No. 50.

    III. PHEBE, b. July 22, 1721. d. unm. October 10, 1738.

    IV. JOSEPH, b. August 4, 1723. m. Abigail Hebard. n. t.

    V. MERCY, b. October 27, 1725. m. John Baker, d. 1814, aged 89 years.

    VI. WILLIAM, b, December 12, 1727. d. unm. February 9, 1743.

    VII. JONATHAN, b. August 24, 1729. d. unm. February 10, 1743.

    VIII. NATHANIEL, b. November 1, 1731. No. 51.

    IV. SAMUEL, b. June 13, 1734. No. 52.

No. 23.

SETH CARY, son of Deacon Joseph, No. 7, b. in Windham, Ct., July 29, 1697 ; resided on his father's farm ; was a member of the First Congregational Church ; a quiet and useful citizen, not active in public affairs.   He was twice married; his first wife was Mary Hebard, m, April 17, 1722, she d. March, 1751 ; and he m. Hannah ———.   He d. 1777, aged 80 years.

His children were :

I.   MARY, b. October 20, 1723. m. James Moulton, jr.

II.   SETH, b. July 12, 1725. m. Hannah Jennings, 1758. n. t.

III.   ELIZABETH, b. April 25, 1727. n. t.

IV.   JOSIAH, b. June 18, 1729. No. 53.

V.   JOANNA, b. December 28, 1731. m. John Frome.

VI.   DANIEL,* b. February 22, 1733.

VII.   ABIGAIL, b. May 15, 1736. n. t.

VIII.   HANNAH, b. June 25, 1789. n. t.

IX.   MOSES,† b. December 15, 1740.

---

*DANIEL, not named in his father's will, and it is probable he d. without issue.

†MOSES, m. and had children among whom were Moses, Ebenezer and Daniel. Ebenezer and Daniel d. young. Their brother Moses m. and had children, among whom were Moses, Ebenezer and Daniel. Ebenezer lives at Schuylkill, N. Y.; Daniel settled in in Niagara Co., N. Y.; and Moses in Connecticut. I regret that I have been unable by correspondence to gather up the family records complete.

Fourth Generation.

No. 24.

ELEAZER CARY, son of Deacon Eleazer, No. 9, b. at Bristol, R. I., November 19, 1713; went with his father to Windham, Ct.; m. Jerusha, daughter of Deacon Nathaniel Wales, January 29, 1736; he d. July 24, 1754, and his widow m. Capt. James Lasell.

His children were:

I. ELEAZER, b. August 7, 1737. No. 54.

II. NATHANIEL, b. January 17, 1739. No. 55.

III. SUSANNAH, b. April 22, 1742. d. July 25, 1754.

IV. ALTHEA, b. April 15, 1744. m. Jonah Smith.

V. PHINEAS, b. October 7, 1746. No. 56.

VI. PRUDENCE, b. March 26, 1749, d. July, 1750.

VII. LYDIA, b. December 26, 1751. d. September 17, 1754.

VIII. JERUSHA, b. January 14, 1755. m. Reuben Welch.

No. 25.

DEACON WILLIAM CARY, son of Deacon Eleazer, No. 9,
b. in Windham, Ct., October 28, 1729; m. Eunice daughter
of Nathaniel Webb, February 19, 1754; resided in Windham
until about 1772, when he removed with his family to Lempster, N. H. He was an unusually large, bony and strong man,
some remarkable stories are recorded of his great strength;
it is said that he could throw barrels of cider into a cart, as
fast as a man could put them on end; in 1761 when a neigh-
bor's house was on fire, he took a tub of water, holding over
a barrel, carried it across four post and rail fences, dashed it
upon the fire and put it out. He was deacon of the church
in Lempster, and a man highly esteemed and of great influence; he d. May 7, 1808, aged 79 years; his wife d. in
1809.

His children were;

I.   SUSANNAH, b. December 11, 1754. d. July 30, 1757.

II. ELEAZER,* b. April 23, 1757.   *d May 15. 1790.*

III. MARY, b. February 20, 1759. m. —— Nichols,
     and had a large family.

IV. OLIVET, b. October 20, 1761. No. 57.

V.   ELLIOTT, b. December 20, 1763. No. 58.

VI. EUNICE,† ⎫ TRIPLETS ⎧
VII. WILLIAM, ⎬ b. January ⎨ No. 59.
VIII. JAMES,   ⎭   4, 1767. ⎩ d. in youth.

*ELEAZER, m. Lavina Willey, had one dau; d. 1790:
†EUNICE, m. — Willey and had 10 children.

IX.   Lydia, b. February 17, 1769. d. May 12, 1770.

X.   Susannah, b. April 14, 1771. m. —— Wait, of
        N. Y.

XI.   Throop, b. 1773. d. 1776.

XII.   Lydia, b. 1775, m. Samuel Ayres, of Pennsyl-
        vania.

XIII.   John F., } Twins   { No. 60.
XIV.   Nancy,* } *(Oct 14* {
                 b. 1777.

XV.   Susan, b. 1779. d. young.

No. 26.

Benjamin Cary, son of Deacon Benjamin, No. 11, b. at
Bristol, R. I., 1706; m. Thankful Taylor, of Plymouth, Mass.,
1733; purchased real estate in Providence, R. I., in 1737 and
resided there; the house in which he lived is still in a good
state of preservation, and is known as " Old Deacon Cary's
House."   He d. in old age, universally esteemed for his purity of character and life.

---

*Nancy, m. Samuel Saxton and had two sons, both d. of cholera, in
Cincinnati, O.

His children were:

    I.   John, b. 1734. n. t.

    II.   Joseph, b. 1736. No. 61.

    III. Thomas, b. 1741. n. t.,

    IV. Nathaniel,* b. 1743.

    V.   Ebenezer, b. 1745. No. 62.

    VI. Thankful, b. 1747. m. James Aplin, Otsego county, N. Y.

    VII. Abigail, b. 1749. m. — Simmons.

    VIII. Susan, b. 1761. m. Henry Vanderbin, Duchess county, N. Y.

    IX. George,† b. 1763.

No. 27.

Allen Cary, son of Deacon Benjamin, No. 11, b. at Bristol, R. I., 1708; m. Hannah Church, October 9, 1731.

---

*Nathaniel, m. Mary Locke, of Duchess county, N. Y. and had one son, Absalom, who never married.

†George went to South Carolina; m. and settled there; have no further trace of him.

His children were :

I.   MOLLY, b. December 3, 1732. n. t.

II. BENJAMIN, b. January 10, 1734. n. t.

III. ABIGAIL, b. December 23, 1736. m. John Field, Providence, R. I.

IV. ALLEN, b. January 1, 1738. d. June 25, 1739.

V.   SUSANNAH, b. August 7, 1740. m. Jonathan Gladding, February 8, 1764.

VI. HANNAH, b. September 26, 1742. m. William Munro, January 9, 1768; her descendants very. numerous; she d. 1834, aged 92 years.

No. 28.

NATHANIEL CARY, son of Deacon Benjamin, No. 11, b. at Bristol, R. I., 1712; m. Elizabeth Warton, of Newport, R. I., August 4, 1740; she d. 1769 and he m. Ama Pearce. He was colonel of a R. I. regiment, and was a distinguished soldier and officer in the war of the Revolution; he was very large and athletic, and of splendid personal appearance. In the cemetery at Bristol is a handsome tomb, erected by his grand-children, bearing this inscription " To the memory of Col. Nathaniel Cary, Esqr., who died September 24, 1784, aged 72 years."

By his will proven in 1784, he gives his estate in Bristol, to his daughter, Mrs. Ellery, and makes bequests to his five grand children; by his will he emancipates his mulatto man " Ichabod " and provides for his support. He had but one child.

  I. Abigail, b. November 12, 1742. She m. William
    Ellery, of Newport, R. I., June 28, 1767.
    Ellery was Governor of the state. She had
    five children, and her numerous descendants
    still live in Rhode Island.

No. 29.

Eleazer Cary, son of Samuel, No. 13, b. in Bridgewater, Mass., 1718; removed with his father and family to Duchess county, N. Y., and thence went as a pioneer to Wyoming valley, Pa., in 1769; he m. a Miss Sturdevant and had a large family of sons and daughters; several of the family lost their lives at the memorable Wyoming. massacre. The place of settlement of this family was called and is still known as Cary town, a few miles from Wilkesbarre. He d. there at an advanced age.

His children were :

   I.   NATHAN, b. 1755. No. 63.

   II.   JOHN,* b, May 7, 1756.

   III.   SAMUEL,† b. 1759.

   IV.   BENJAMIN,‡ b. 1761.

   V.   COMFORT,‡ b. 1763.

   VI.   MEHITABEL,§ b. 1765.

*JOHN CARY, was a man of herculean frame, marvelous strength and great-personal courage. He enlisted under Capt. Durkee, in the Revolutionary war and served with distinction throughout the war; was at the Wyoming massacre and escaped death. It is recorded of him, that when 18 years of age, when the early settlers of the valley were suffering for food, he went on foot over the mountains in the severe cold of winter to Easton for flour. Some of his descendants still remain in . the Wyoming Valley and others are widely scattered. The writer has failed to group his descendants. He d. 1844, aged 88 years and is buried at Wilkesbarre; his wife, Susannah. d. 1815, aged 71 years.

†SAMUEL CARY was small in stature, but active, energetic, persevering and patriotic. He was in the Battle of Wyoming under Capt. Bidlock and was among those who escaped massacre; he was taken prisoner by the Indians and remained a captive for six years; he was supposed to have been murdered but unexpectedly returned in 1784 to Wyoming, having suffered incredible hardships for six long years; he m. Susanna, a daughter of Capt. Daniel Gore, and lived and died in Wyoming Valley; he d. 1843, aged 84 years.

‡BENJAMIN AND COMFORT CARY, both lived and died in Cary-town; they were men of wealth and influence; lived to old age, but I have no authentic trace of their families. Benjamin had a daughter who m. Bateman Downing and lived in Wisconsin.

§MEHITABEL, m. James Wright, in Lucerne county, Pa. and had numerous descendants.

No.30.

Ezra Cary, son of Ephraim, No. 14, b. in Bridgewater, Mass., 1710; m. Mary, a daughter of John Holman, 1734; removed to the state of New Jersey, and afterwards to western Pennsylvania, where he d. 1778.

His children were :

    I.   Ezra, b. 1735. No. 64.

    II. Luther,* b. 1737.

    III. Calvin,* b. 1739.

    IV. Ephraim, b. 1741. d. uum. at New Orleans.

No. 31.

Zechariah Cary, son of Ephraim, No. 14, b. in Bridgewater, Mass., 1713; m. Susanna, a daughter of Capt. Jonathan Bass, in 1742, and settled in N. Bridgewater, where he d. 1788, aged 75 years.

His children were :

    I.   Ezra, b. 1749. No. 65.

    II. Mehitabel,† b. 1752.

    III. Susanna,‡ b. 1755.

    IV. Daniel, b. June 11, 1758. No. 66.

    V. Luther, b. 1761. No. 67.

*Luther and Calvin are supposed to have descendants residing in the western states, but it is impossible to trace them.

†Mehitabel, m. Zechariah Silvester, and removed to Raymond, Me.

‡Susanna, m. Rufus Britt, 1775, and removed to Paris, Me.

No. 32.

EPHRAIM CARY, son of Ephraim, No. 14, b. in Bridge-water, Mass., 1714; m. Susanna, daughter of Ebenezer Alden; settled in Bridgewater, where he d. 1791, aged 77 years; his wife d. 1803, aged 85 years.

His children were:

 I. ANNA, b. 1739. d. unm. 1804.

 II. AZULAH, b. 1741. m. Josiah Johnson, and d. 1816.

 III. PHEBE,* b. 1742.

 IV. EPHRAIM, b. 1748. No. 68.

 V. SUSANNA, b. 1750. m. Asa Keith.

 VI. HULDAH, b. 1752. m. Simeon Allen.

 VII. DANIEL,† b. 1754.

No. 33.

DANIEL CARY, son of Ephraim, No. 14, b. in Bridge-water, Mass., 1716; m. Martha, daughter of John Cary, 1742; had one son, b. in Bridgewater, and removed to New Jersey; bought a large farm extending from Black river eastward, running up the mountain slope on Suckasunny Plains, Morris county, where he d. at an advanced age.

---

*PHEBE, m. Ezra Alden and had eleven children; one of her sons, Ethan Alden, graduated at Middlebury College, Vermont, and was an Episcopalian Minister in Washington City.

†DANIEL, m. Hannah Thayer, but had no children.

His children were:

    I.   LEWIS, b. 1742. No. 69.

    II.   ABEL,* b. 1744.

    III.   HANNAH,† b. April 26, 1747.

    IV.   POLLY, b. 1749. m. Usual Cary, of Catskill, N. Y.

    V.   PHEBE, b. 1751, m. James Cooper.

No. 34.

ICHABOD CARY, son of Recompence, No. 16, b. in Bridge-water, Mass., 1715 ; m. Hannah, daughter of Joseph Jannett, 1741 ; and afterwards removed, cannot learn where.

His children were:

    I.   SETH, b. 1747. Went to Putney, Vt.

    II.   ICHABOD,‡ b. 1749.

    III.   AARON, b. April 6, 1751. No. 70.

    IV.   JOSHUA, b. 1753. n. t.

    V.   ZENOS, b. 1755. n. t.

    VI.   HANNAH, b. 1758. m. — Coloph, of Gen. Burgoyne's Army.

    VII.   MARY, b. 1761. n. t.

    VIII.   DANIEL, b. 1762. n. t.

    IX.   EBENEZER, b. 1765. n. t.

*ABEL CARY, m. and went to Redstone, near Washington, Pa., where he d. in 1820. No trace of his descendants.

†HANNAH, m. — Thompson, an eminent Judge in New Jersey.

‡ICHABOD, m. — Smith, and had four sons and a daughter in Colerain, Mass.

It is supposed that most of this family removed to Nova Scotia or Canada, or d. in the Revolutionary War.

No. 35.

Col. Simeon Cary, son of Recompence, No. 16, b. in Bridgewater, Mass, 1719; was a Captain in the French war of 1758-9, and a Colonel in the Revolutionary war; was a man of distinction and influence; he m. Mary, daughter of Daniel Howard, 1754. He d. in Bridgewater, 1802, aged 83 years.

His children were:

I. Molly, b. 1755. m. Simeon Keith, 1775.

II. Mehitabel, b. 1757. m. Bela Howard, 1782.

III. Hovard, b. 1760. No. 71.

IV. Martha, b. 1765. m. Benjamin Keith, 1788.

V. Rhoda, b. 1772. m. Richard Wild, 1794.

No. 36.

Zebulon Cary, son of Recompence, No. 16, b. in Bridgewater, Mass., 1721; m. Mehitabel, daughter of Matthew Janett 1747; she d. 1748; and he m. Lydia Phillips, 1749; he d. at Ward, Mass., 1759.

His children were:

I. Mehitabel, b. 1751. · m. Joseph Allen, 1771.

II. Lydia, b 1753. m. —— Thomas, and went to Ward, Mass.

III. Josiah, b. 1754. No. 72.

IV. Zebulon, b. 1755. Lost at sea. unm.

V. Recompence, b. January 25, 1757. No. 73.

VI. Mary, b. 1758. m. —— Oaks, of Hawley, Mass.

No. 37.

JONATHAN CARY, son of Recompence, No. 16, b. in Bridgewater, Mass., 1723; m. Mary, daughter of Capt. Joseph Curtis, of Staughton, Mass., 1747. He was remarkable for his probity and exalted Christian character. He was a member of the Congregational Church in Bridgewater for 70 years; was a deacon for 60. He lived with his companion for 65 years; and d. February 2, 1813, aged 90 years; his wife d. at 95 years.

His children were:

I. MOSES, b. November 20, 1748.   No. 74.

II. MARY, b. 1750.   d. 1768.

III. DOROTHY, b. December 17, 1752.   d. a maiden.

IV. JONATHAN, b. February 14, 1757.   No. 75.

V. HULDAH, b. 1759.   d. 1763.

VI. ALPHEUS, b. April 21, 1761.   No. 76.

VII. HULDAH, b. August 4, 1763.   d. 1775.

VIII. SARAH,* b. 1765.

IX. JAMES, b. 1766.   No. 77.

No. 38.

JOHN CARY, son of John No. 17, b. in Bridgewater, Mass., 1719; m. Mary Hardin in 1741, and after the birth of his two eldest children, removed to Mendham, Morris county,

---

*SARAH was twice m. first to Daniel Alden, 1786; and second to L. A. Beal, 1809.

N. J. He was a carpenter, and built the first place of worship in Mendham. He lived at the foot of the hill, east of the church, on a large farm. His first wife d. February 6, 1785; and he m. Elizabeth Riggs, Feb. 6, 1786. He d. August 20, 1793, aged 72 years.

His children were:

    I.   Isaac, b. February 1, 1742. No. 78.

    II.   Huldah, b. March, 1744. m — Hedley, in Pennsylvania.

    III.   Susanna, b. May 8, 1746. m. Clement Wood, of New Jersey.

    IV.   Eunice, b. February 5, 1751. m. N. Wade, in Sussex county, N. J.

    V.   Martha, b. February 26, 1753. d. January 28, 1762.

    VI.   John, b. July 25, 1757. . No. 79.

    VII.   Sarah, b. March 8, 1760. m. Daniel Baxter, of Pennsylvania.

No. 39.

Henry Cary, son of John, No. 17, b. in Bridgewater, Mass., 1723; m. Martha, daughter of Joseph Byrom, 1749; settled in Bridgewater, where he d. 1762.

His children were:

   I.   BENJAMIN, b. 1750.   Killed accidentally.

  II.   EUNICE, b. 1758. m. Wm. Snell, 1781.

 III.   BENJAMIN, b. 1761.   Supposed to have died young. Name extinct.

No. 40.

BERIAH CARY, son of John, No. 17, b. in Bridgewater, Mass., 1729; m. a Miss Cook, by whom he had four children; she d. and he m. Jane Rogers, by whom he had five children. He removed with his brother John, to Morris county, N. J., where he d.

His children were:

    I.   JOEL, b. 1758. n. t.

   II.   STEPHEN, b. 1760.   Was a printer in Philadelphia.

  III.   THANKFUL, } TWINS { n. t.

  IV.   HANNAH, } b. 1764. { m. Thos. Homan.

   V.   DANIEL, b. 1768. n. t.

  VI.   SAMUEL, b. 1770. n. t.

 VII.   REUBEN, b. 1772. n. t.

VIII.   SIMEON, b. 1774. n. t.

  IX.   REBECCA, b. 1776. n. t.

No. 41.

ELEAZER CARY, son of Jonathan, No. 18, b. in Bridgewater, Mass,, 1723. m. first, Betty, daughter of Jonathan
Fobes, 1745, by whom he had one son. This wife d. 1749,
and he m. Mary, widow of Nathaniel Washburne, 1753. He
d. 1806, aged 83 years.

His children were ;

 I. CALEB, b. 1747. n. t.

 II. BETTY, b. 1754. m. William Perkins, 1777.

 III. MARY,* b. 1756.

 IV. SARAH b. 1761. d. unm.

No. 42.

JONATHAN CARY, son of Jonathan, No. 18, b. in Bridgewater, Mass., 1730. m. Lois, daughter of William Hooper,
Esqr., 1754, and lived and d. in Bridgewater.

His children were :

 I. JONATHAN, b. 1754. d. in the army of "Camp
  Ail."

 II. LOIS, ⎱ TWINS, ⎰ m. Solomon Keith, 1777.

 III. EUNICE, ⎰ b. 1760. ⎱ m. Isaac Washburne.

The name became extinct in this branch by the death of
Jonathan, in the Revolutionary war; unm.

 *MARY, m. Nathan Morton, Esqr., 1782; and was the mother of Judge
Marcus Morton.

No. 43.

Michael Cary, son of David, No. 19, b. in Bristol, R. I., January 24, 1739.   m. Patty Gunsey, in Barrington, Mass. He was a soldier in the Revolutionary war, and a pensioner at the time of his death.   He d. 1833, aged 94 years.

His children were:

    I. Ebenezer, b. about 1761. No. 80.

    II. Nathan, b. about 1767.   d. without issue.

    III. Mary, b. about 1769.   d. without issue.

No. 44.

Thomas Cary, son of David, No. 19, b. in Bristol, R. I., January 19, 1735; was by occupation a cabinet maker.   He was m. in Smithfield, R. I., about 1764, to Sarah, daughter of Obediah Brown, of Gloucester, R. I., a large landholder, and a descendant of Elder Chad. Brown, one of the original proprietors of the Providence Purchase, he having been exiled from Massachusetts with Roger Williams.

Their children were:

    I. Ebenezer,* b. 1765.

    III. Chad., b. May 17, 1773.   No. 81.

    III. Asa, b. about 1775. n. t.

    IV. Sally, b. about 1777. n. t.

*Ebenezer was a sailor, and near the close of the Revolutionary war he was pressed on board of an English war vessel, and died in a prison ship.

No. 45.

JOSEPH CARY, son of Jabez, No. 21, b. in Windham Ct., September 28, 1723 ; m. Phebe Mack, July 1, 1747 ; lived in Windham for a time ; removed to Mansfield, Ct., and thence to Williamsburg, Mass., about 1765, where he d.

His children were:

    I.   HANNAH,* b. June 11, 1748.

    II.   PHEBE,† b. January 6, 1750.

    III.   MARY,‡ b. December 5, 1751.

    IV.   JEMIMA,§ b. November 21, 1753.

    V.   ELIZABETH,‖ b. March 10, 1755.

    VI.   JOSEPH, b. March 7, 1757.   No. 82.

    VII.   RICHARD, b. January 15, 1759.   No. 83.

    VIII.   ABNER, b. January 21, 1760.   No. 84.

    IX.   TRIPHENA, b. December 11, 1763.   n. t.

    X.   A daughter b. in Williamsburg, Mass.

    XI.   A daughter b. in Williamsburg, Mass.

    XII.   ASA, b. April 1, 1770.   No. 85.

*HANNAH m. Thomas Meekens, July 1767, had two sons; she d. at Williamsburg, Mass., aged 80 years.

†PHEBE m. Amasa Graves, July 13, 1769; had fourteen children, and d. at Middlefield, Mass., August 3, 1815, aged 65.

‡MARY m. Joel Wait, had five children; d. in Ohio, in 1836, aged 85 years.

§JEMIMA m. John Ford, 1771; had eight children, and d. at Middlefield, Mass., September, 1849, aged 96 years.

‖ELIZABETH m. Anson Cheesman, 1774, had eight children; d. in Freedonia, N. Y., October 12, 1841, aged 89 years.

No. 46.

JABEZ CARY, son of Jabez, No. 21, b. in Windham, Ct.,
July 30, 1727; lived for some years in Mansfield, and then
removed, it is believed, to Oneida county, N. Y., and the
Carys of Oneida are undoubtedly descended from this ancestor.

His children were:

    I.   JABEZ, b. October 3, 1760.

    II.   LYDIA, b. September 10, 1762.

   III.   BELA,* b. December 2, 1764.

   IV.   JAMES, b. April 4, 1766.

    V.   MARTHA, b. January 3, 1770.

   VI.   SAMUEL, b. May 2, 1772.

  VII.   LUCY, b. July 5, 1774.

 VIII.   OLIVE, b. July 25, 1776.

   IX.   RICHARD, b. November 22, 1778.

No distinct trace of this family.

No. 47.

NATHANIEL CARY, son of Jabez, No. 21, b. in Windham,
Ct., October 23, 1729; resided in Mansfield, Ct., for a time
and removed I can not learn where.   He m. first, Dorcas,
daughter of Samuel Marcy, of Woodstock, Ct., September
12, 1751; she bore him seven children, and d. December 13,
1766.   He m. second, Sarah, daughter of Jacob Sargent, De-

---

*BELA m. in Oneida county, N. Y., had a family, all of whom are
dead.

cember, 1767, by whom he had six children, and d. August 11, 1782. He m. third, *widow* Tabitha Root, of Willington, Ct., March 18, 1784, by whom he had two children. He lived to a very old age.

His children were :

     I.   MARY, b. July 16, 1752. n. t.

    II.   DELIGHT, b. September 6, 1754. m. Timothy Fuller, June 14, 1774.

   III. DORCAS, b. July 11, 1756. n. t.

   IV. NATHANIEL,* b. April 18, 1758.

    V.   LUCRETIA, b. October 2, 1760. n. t.

   VI. SIBBEL, b. October 11, 1762. n. t.

  VII. SARAH, b. October 1, 1764. n. t.

 VIII. JERUSHA, b. November 5, 1768. n. t.

   IX. HANNAH, b. July 5, 1770. n. t.

    X.   BARILLAI, b. March 5, 1772. n. t.

   XI. ASA, b. February 11, 1774. n. t.

  XII. JOHN, b. May 11, 1777. n. t.

 XIII. ELEAZER, b. May 15, 1779. n. t.

 XIV. PROSPER, b. February 7, 1785. n. t.

  XV. PERSIS, b. March 15, 1786. n. t.

It is somewhat strange that I have found no trace of this large family. It is hoped that some of the descendants may see this and complete their family records.

---

*NATHANIEL enlisted in the Continental army, May 12, 1777, for three years, and lost his life in the service.

No. 48.

EBENEZER CARY, son of Jabez, No. 21, b. in Mansfield, Ct., 1732; m. Sarah, daughter of Walter Trumbull, March 30, 1758; lived in Chaplin, (part of Mansfield). He was a a deacon of the church many years, and was universally esteemed for his probity and pure character. He d. March 16, 1816, aged 84 years; his wife d. August 18, 1830, aged 89 years.

His children were:

I. EBENEZER, b. December 27, 1758. No. 86.

II. SARAH,* b. May 25, 1761.

III. WALTER TRUMBULL,† b. August, 1762.

IV. LUCINDA,‡ b. September 6, 1765.

V. NATHAN,‖ b. 1767.

VI. DAMARIS,§ b. 1769.

VII. ELIZABETH,(a) b. 1772.

VIII. ALFRED,(b) b. 1778.

IX. ELSIE, b. 1782. d. young.

X. TRUMBULL, b. 1787. No. 87.

*SARAH m. Ephraim Gradt, of Toland, Ct., and had five children.

†WALTER TRUMBULL, d. in Carolina, unm. in 1786.

‡LUCINDA, m. W. Kemberly, and had three children; and d. February 17, 1832.

‖NATHAN, was educated at Brown University, for the ministry; never m. and d. in Georgia.

§DAMARIS, m. E. Williams, Toland, Ct., and d. without issue.

(a)ELIZABETH, m. John Foote, of Toland, Ct., had two children; and d. December 13, 1852.

(b)ALFRED, never m. He founded the "Cary Institute," at Dahpela, N. Y., and gave it an endowment of $20,000; and erected two fine substantial stone buildings for the Institute; and d. September 17, 1858.

No. 49.

JOHN CÁRY, son of John, No. 22, b. in Windham, Ct., April 12, 1717; was a very prominent and influential man in "Scotland Parish." He m. Rebecca, daughter of Nathaniel Rudd, November 13, 1740. He d. May 8, 1788; his widow d. 1797.

His children were :

I. EZEKIEL, b. December 7, 1741. No. 88.

II. PHEBE, b. November 14, 1743. d. unm.

III. HANNAH, b. November 15, 1745. d. unm.

IV. WILLIAM, b. October 25, 1747. No. 89.

V. JONATHAN, b. June 5, 1749. No. 90.

VI. JOHN, b. August 9, 1751. d. Sept. 29, 1776. unm.

VII. REBECCA, b. December 29, 1753. m. Walter Baker and had family.

VIII. ESTHER, b. May 14, 1756. d. July 16, 1777. unm.

No. 50.

LIEUT. BENIJAH CARY, son of John, No. 22, b. in Scotland, Ct., March 7, 1719; was a farmer, and very highly esteemed. He m. Deborah Perkins, February 11, 1742. He d. March 11, 1773. She d. December 5, 1772.

His children were:

   I.   Z<small>ILLAH</small>,* b. December 1743.

   II. A<small>NNA</small>, b. February 14, 1745. d. June 19, 1763.

  III. D<small>EBORAH</small>, b. February 17, 1747. m. —— Stark, of Franklin, Ct., and had children.

  IV. J<small>AMES</small>, b. November 27, 1750. No. 91.

   V. M<small>ARTHA</small>, b. May 18, 1755. d. June 2, 1762.

  VI. A<small>BIGAIL</small>, b. July 27, 1758. d. June 8, 1772.

No. 51.

C<small>APT</small>. N<small>ATHANIEL</small> C<small>ARY</small>, son of John, No. 22, b. in Scotland, Ct., November 1, 1731; was a prominent and much esteemed farmer; was a captain in the early part of the Revolutionary war. He m. Jerusha Downer, January 6, 1757. He d. November 22, 1776; his widow lived to be over 90 years old.

*Z<small>ILLAH</small>, m. Jonathan Kingsley, and was the mother of Prof. Luce Kingsley, of Yale College.

His children were:

I. IRENA, b. October 2, 1757. d. January 7, 1777. unm.

II. ROGER, b. January 7, 1759. No. 92.

III. JOSEPH,* b. August 19, 1760.

IV. ANSON, b. March 15, 1762. No. 93.

V. MARTHA,† b. January 13, 1764.

VI. LAVINA, b. September 23, 1765. m. Asa Parish, of Vermont.

VII. PHILOMELA,‡ b. March 2, 1767.

No. 52.

SAMUEL CARY, son of John, No. 22, b. in Scotland, Ct., June 13, 1734; graduated at Yale College, in the class of 1755, (his diploma is in the possession of his grandson Samuel F. Cary, at College Hill). He was a physician of eminent skill; he m. Deliverance Grant, who was born in Bolton, Ct., May 23, 1743; m. January 7, 1762, and emigrated to Lyme, N. H., 1768. He d. at Lyme, January, 1784; and his grave-stone may be found in the old burying ground on the hill, near the Connecticut river, long since abandoned as a burial place. His widow m. Capt. John Strong, of Thetford, Vt., and had by him two sons, John, b. March 25, 1787; and Zebulon, b. September 7, 1788. Becoming a widow the

---

*JOSEPH, was a sea captain, and was engaged in the slave trade; he d. on the coast of Africa; was never m.

†MARTHA, m. Benjamin Greenslit, and had four children.

‡PHILOMELA, m. Josiah Geer; had a family and d. in old age in Illinois.

second time, she emigrated to Cincinnati, O., in 1802, with her children, Christopher, Samuel, Delia and William. She d. at the old Cary mansion, at the junction of Main street and Hamilton Road, in 1810; and was buried where the First Presbyterian Church now stands, at the corner of Fourth and Main streets, Cincinnati. John and Zebulon Strong, emigrated to Ohio in 1809, and both had large families. John d. at 83; Zebulon still lives at College Hill, aged 85 years.

His children were:

   I.   CHRISTOPHER, b. February 25, 1763.   No. 94.

  II. ANNA.* b. May 5, 1765.

 III. PHEBE,† b. August 25, 1767.

 IV. DELIVERANCE, b. Oct. 26, 1769.   d. unm in 1828.

  V. HANNAH, b. December 16, 1771.   d. in infancy.

 VI. SAMUEL, b. 1773.   d. in infancy.

VII. MERCY,‡ b. March 5, 1776.

VIII. SAMUEL,‖ b. November 3. 1778.

 IX. JOHN, b. December 26, 1780.   No. 95.

  X. WILLIAM, b. January 28, 1783.   No. 96.

*ANNA, m. Solomon Howard, a Revolutionary soldier in Lyme, N. H., removed with four children to Cincinnati, Ohio, in 1806. She d. at College Hill, 1854, aged 89 years. Her descendants are very numerous among whom are two sons, Rev. Solomon Howard, D. D., long President of Ohio University, and the Hon. R. F. Howard, of Xenia, O.

†PHEBE, m. at Lyme, N. H., to John Crary, in 1783; had a numerous family; removed to Cincinnati, O., in 1806. She d. in 1822. Lyman Crary, of College Hill, now 87 years old, is a son, and the Rev. B. F. Crary, D. D., formerly President of Wisconsin University, now editor of Christian Advocate (Methodist), of St. Louis, is a grandson.

‡MERCY, m. Thomas Weston, of Townsend, Mass., had a large family; her descendants are scattered from Ohio to Oregon. She emigrated with family to Ohio, in 1828; and d. in 1830, at College Hill.

‖SAMUEL CARY, emigrated to Cincinnati, in 1802; was the first merchant tailor in the town; and d. unm. of small pox, in 1804.

No. 53.

JOSIAH CARY, son of Seth, No. 23, b. in Windham, Ct., June 18, 1729; removed to Haddam, Ct. m. 1760, to Hannah Conklin.

His children were:

I. JOSIAH, b. January 16, 1761. No. 97.

II. POLLY, b. 1763. m. —— Doan.

III. BETSEY, b. 1765. m. John Strong.

IV. THANKFUL, b. 1767. m. —— Harden.

V. HANNAH, b. 1769. m. first, Daniel Brainerd; second, W. Johnson.

Fifth Generation.

No. 54.

ELEAZER CARY, son of Eleazer, No. 24, b. in Windham, Ct., August 7, 1737; m. Mercy Lathrop, widow of John Fitch, July 19, 1767. He kept a popular hotel in Windham, during the Revolutionary war, until his death August 21, 1782. His widow kept the hotel for many years after his death; she d. October 2, 1802.

He had but one child:

    I. HENRY LUCIUS, b. October 18, 1769. No. 98.

No. 55.

NATHANIEL CARY, son of Eleazer, No. 24, b. in Windham Ct., January 17, 1739; m. Zervia, daughter of Thomas Storrs, in Mansfield, Ct., December 5, 1765; lived for some years in Mansfield, where all his children were born; but d. in Windham, 1818; his widow lived to over 80 years.

His children were:

I.   CLARISSA,* b. January 1, 1767.

II. ELEAZER, b. December 14, 1769. No. 99.

III. ZERVIA, b. February 6, 1772. d. March 24, 1786.

No. 56.

PHINEAS CARY, son of Eleazer, No. 24, b. Windham, Ct., October 7, 1746; m. Mary, daughter of Elisha Hurlbut, February 26, 1769. He emigrated to the state of New York.

His children were:

I.   MARY, b. March 20, 1770.   n. t.

II. ANNE, b. October 26, 1771.   n. t.

III. ELISHA, b. August 12, 1775.   n. t.

*CLARISSA, m. Benjamin Bibbins, December 31, 1789; had a family. She d. January 19, 1860, aged 93 years.

No. 57.

OLIVET CARY, son of Deacon William, No. 25, b. in Windham, Ct., October 20, 1761; removed with his father to Lempster, N. H. He m. Bertha Woods, about 1790. He d. at Lempster, in 1833; his widow lived until 1845.

His children were:

I. AMANDA,* b. May 7, 1791.

II. EUNICE,† b. August 17, 1793.

III. SOPHRONIA,‡ b. October 10, 1795.

IV. DEBORAH,|| b. January 26, 1798.

V. FANNY, b. Nov. 12, 1801. m. Oliver Newell, 1847.

VI. BERTHA, b. February 11, 1803. m. W. S. Bools.

VII. MARY ANN, b. 1806. m. —— Winship, in Erie county, N. Y.

VIII. OLIVET, b. November 6, 1810. No. 100.

No. 58.

ELLIOTT CARY, son of Deacon William, No. 25, b. in Windham, Ct.; removed with parents to Lempster, N. H., was a respectable farmer; m. Anna Roundy, August 8, 1790; have no record of his death.

*AMANDA, m. B. A. Miner, January 27, 1811; was living in New Hampshire at last account; had four daughters and one son; the latter lives in Buffalo, New York.

†EUNICE, m. Amasa Loveridge, 1815; had six sons and two daughters; and when last heard from was living a widow in Buffalo, New York.

‡SOPHRONIA, m. Anson Wheeler; had two sons and one daughter living at Coryden, New Hampshire.

||DEBORAH, m. John Wheeler, 1823; had one daughter, and d. 1833.

His children were:

    I.   LUCINDA, b. December 12, 1792. unm.

    II.   ELLIOTT,* b. 1794.

    III.   LYDIA, b. August 17, 1786. unm.

    IV.   NANCY, b. February 17, 1799. d. April 3, 1812.

    V.   ALDEN, b. 1801. No 101.

    VI.   JOHN, b. February, 1804. d. unm.

    VII.   ISEMIRAH, b. 1806. d. 1812.

    VIII.   WILLARD, b. September 3, 1810. d. 1812.

    IX.   SUSANNA, b. August 13, 1813. d. October 5, 1850. Left two children.

No. 59.

WILLIAM CARY, son of Deacon William, No. 25, b. in Windham, Ct., January 4, 1767; removed with parents to Lempster, N. H., was a farmer; m. Jerusha Sabin, March 14, 1795. He d. at Lempster, January 9, 1815.

ELLIOTT, m. Sally Fletcher, 1820; lives at Lempster, N. H. No issue.

His children were:

    I.   WILLIAM, b. February 12, 1796. No. 102.

   II.   JERUSHA, b. September 9, 1797. d. at Unity, N.
           H., 1837.

 III.   BYFIELD, b. November 25, 1799. No. 103.

 IV.   HARVEY, b. May 10, 1802. No. 104.

  V.   PERMELIA, b. July 10, 1804. 'd. at Lempster,
           1836.

 VI.   MINERVA,* b. January 15, 1807.

VII.   JOHN, b. June 12, 1810. No. 105.

VIII. WEALTHY,† b. June 25, 1814.

No. 60.

JOHN F. CARY, son of Deacon William, No. 25, b. in Lempster, N. H., 1777; was educated at Dartmouth College, graduated in the class of 1800; removed to Alexandria, N. Y., m. Esther Stanton, in 1804, and then removed to Meadville, Pa.; was engaged in the business of teaching a number of years, and finally settled on a farm in Chatauque county, N. Y., and d. suddenly September 28, 1828.

    *MINERVA, m. John Wellman, M. D., and d. at Ravenna, O., 1843.
    †WEALTHY, m. Nicholas E. Sargent, 1832. d. at Acworth, N. H., July 28, 1862.

His children were:

I.   FERDINAND F.,* b. November 9, 1805.

II.   WILLIAM D.,* b. September 7, 1807.

III.   DANIEL H.,* b. August 13, 1809.

IV.   ESTHER D.,† b. 1811.

No. 61.

JOSEPH CARY, son of Deacon Benjamin, No. 26, b. in Bristol, R. I., 1736; went when a child, with his parents to Providence, R. I.; m. first, Ruth Carew, 1763, by whom he had three children; his wife d. June 24, 1769, and he m. second, Zeruah Hutchins, of Killingly, Ct., January 8, 1772; removed to Plainfield, Ct., and had by second wife, seven children. He afterwards removed to Richfield, Saratoga county, N. Y., where he d. in 1818; his wife d. 1828.

*These sons with families reside in Chatauque county, N. Y, but cannot get records.

†ESTHER, m. —— Fowler, and had two sons and a daughter; both sons d. in the Union army, in the war of the rebellion. She lives at Warrensville, Dupage county, Illinois.

His children were:

I. ELIZABETH, b. August 28, 1764. m. —— Hicks, of Providence, R. I.

II. SAMUEL, b. August 18, 1766. No. 106.

III. RUTH, b. June 13, 1769. n. t.

IV. JOSEPH, b. August 18, 1773. No. 107.

V. KEZIA, b. July 31, 1775. d. January 18, 1790.

VI. DARIUS H., b. March 24, 1777. No. 108.

VII. WILLIAM, b. April 12, 1778. No. 109.

VIII. NABA, b. April 9, 1782. d. October 10, 1813, at Plainfield, Ct.

IX. EZRA, b. August 25, 1785. No. 110.

X. AUGUSTUS, b. February 2, 1788. d. without issue at Middlefield, N. Y., 1857.

No. 62.

EBENEZER CARY, son of Deacon Benjamin, No. 26, b. in Providence, R. I., 1745; was educated at Brown University; became an eminent physician. He m. first, Mary Bentley, October 9, 1766; removed to Beekman, Duchess Co., N. Y., and had five children. His wife d. and he m. second, Delight Champlin, November 30th, 1777, and had by her nine children. He was of decided talents, and great professional skill. He represented Duchess county in the Legislature in 1781 and '84; he d. 1815.

His children were:

I. HEPZIBAH, b. January 9, 1767. m. John Smith, Saratoga county, N. Y.

II. LYDIA, b. August 27 1768. m. Rufus Sweet, Beekman, N. Y.

III. WILLIAM, b. November 22, 1769. No. 111.

IV. TAYLOR,. b. March 3, 1778. No. 112.

V. LUCIUS, b. December 27, 1775. d. in infancy.

VI. MATILDA, b. November 14, 1778. m. William Aiken, Greenbush, N. Y.

VII. CYNTHIA, b. November 17, 1780. m. Joseph Arnold.

VIII. DELIGHT, b. July 5, 1783. d. May 26, 1787.

IX. SOPHIA, b. June 16, 1784. d. in infancy.

X. MARIA, b. October 20, 1787. m. Israel Cook.

XI. EGBERT, b. April 12, 1789. No. 113.

XII. HELEN, b. April 27, 1792. m. Silas Germand, Poughkeepsie, N. Y.

XIII. STURGES, b. July 25, 1794. No. 114.

XIV. JAMES ROGERS, b. February 1, 1798. n. t.

No. 63.

NATHAN CARY, son of Eleazer, No. 29, b. in Duchess county, N. Y., 1755; was a man six feet in height, of a very muscular and powerful frame. He was an early emigrant

with his father and brothers to the wilderness of Pennsylvania ;
he was in the memorable battle of Wyoming, but escaped
miraculously and without injury.   He was a soldier in the
Revolutionary war; m. Jane Mann, July 11, 1782, and settled
at Hanover, in Wyoming Valley, until 1779, when he removed to the head waters of the Canisteo river, a place now
known as Arkport, Steuben county, N. Y., purchased a farm
then covered with heavy timber, but he made of it a beautiful
home.   He d. there in 1835, aged 80 years.

His children were :

    I.   JOHNSON, b. March 5, 1783.   No. 115.

    II.   ELEAZER, b. about 1785.   No. 116.

    III.   WILLIAM, b. about 1787.   No. 117.

    IV.   ADAM,* b. about 1789.

    V.   CHRISTOPHER, b. about 1791.   No. 118.

No. 64.

EZRA CARY, son of Ezra, No. 30, b. in Morris county,
N. J., 1735 ; m. Lyda Thompson, and removed to Western
Pennsylvania in 1777; thence with the first settlers to Marietta, Ohio, and thence to Shelby county, Ohio, where he d.
1828, aged 93.

*ADAM, d. unm. at Natchez, Miss., 1825.

His children were:

I. PHEBE, b. 1771. m, —— Harris. d. in Coshocton, county, Ohio.

II. RUFUS,* b. 1773.

III. CEPHAS, b. 1775. No.·119.

IV. EPHRAIM, b. about 1777. Lived in Indiana.

V. ABSALOM, b. about 1782. d. young.

VI. ELIAS, b. about 1786. Lived in Lasalle county, Illinois.

VII. GEORGE, b. about 1793. No. 120.

No. 65.

EZRA CARY, son of Zechariah, No. 31, b. in Bridgewater, Mass., 1749; m. Cynthia Brett, in Staughton, Mass., 1770; and after the birth of two children, removed with his family to Turner, Maine. His wife d. and he m. a Tolman, about 1776. He was a farmer and highly respected.

---

*RUFUS, had a large family, now widely scattered; John Cary of Putnam county, was a son. I have tried to gather up the records of these sons of Ezra, but with poor success. Rufus lived to old age.

His children were:

    I.   THOMAS, b. 1771. No. 121.

   II.   ZACHARY, b. 1773. No. 122.

  III.   LUTHER, b. 1777. d. 1860, aged 83.

  IV.   EZRA, b. 1780. No. 123.

   V.   DANIEL, b. 1784. d. unm.

  VI.   JOHN SHEPHERD, b. 1790. No. 124.

 VII.   CYNTHIA, b. 1792. d. in infancy.

VIII.   BETHUEL, b. 1793. No. 125.

  IX.   TOLMAN, b. 1796. d. uum.

   X.   CYNTHIA, b. 1798. m. —— Newhall, in Turner, Maine.

  XI.   SUSANNA, b. 1800. m. —— Dresser, in Turner, Maine.

No. 66.

MAJOR DANIEL CARY, son of Zachariah, No. 31, b. in Bridgewater, Mass., June 11, 1758; m. Mehitabel, daughter of Simeon Brett, and about 1800, removed to Turner, Maine, where he d. 1819.

His children were :

I.   ZEBIAH, b. July 31, 1779. m. Capt. Roger Sum-
     .ner, 1801.

II. EUNICE, b. September 10, 1781. m. G. Blake,
     in Turner, Maine, 1804.

III. OLIVE, b. April 18, 1783. m. Apollos Howard,
     1802.

IV. FRANCIS, b. May 5, 1785. · No. 126.

V.   JAMES, } b. August 28, 1787. { d. in infancy.
VI. JOHN, }   { d. in infancy.

VII. ZACHARY, b. April 1, 1791. d. November 1, 1800.

VIII. DANIEL, b. September 3, 1793. d. November
     .27, 1795.

IX. AVEY, b. February 15, 1795. m. Dr. R. Bradfort,
     Auburn, Maine, July 5, 1855.

No. 67.

LUTHER CARY, son of Zachary, No. 31, b. in Bridgewater, Mass., 1761 ; studied medicine ; m. Miss Abigail King,
of Raynham, Mass., removed to Oxford county, Maine ; was
a man of considerable distinction, and was for years a judge
of the court. He d. July 12, 1848, aged 87 years. His wife
d. May 30, 1837, aged 76 years.

His children were :

 I. CASSANDER, b. 1782. No. 127.

 II. WILLIAM, b. March 14, 1784. No. 128.

 III. SOPHIA, b. November 17, 1785. m. Dr. Silas
   Blake, 1809; a widow in Harrison, Maine.

 IV. ANSLEM, b. June 8, 1787. No. 129.

 V. EMILY, b. 1788. m. Stephen Pollard, 1809; a
   widow in Livermore, Maine.

 VI. ALANSON, b. December 23, 1790. No. 130.

 VII. HUGH, b. October 17, 1792. No. 131.

 VIII. MAURICE, b. November 15, 1795. No. 132.

 IX. HARRISON, b. 1797. d. in infancy.

 X. CLARA, b. October 1799. · m. Rev. J. P. Richardson. d. 1831 ; left three children.

 XI. LUTHER, b. 1801. d. in infancy.

 XII. NABBY, b. 1803. d. in infancy.

No. 68.

EPHRAIM CARY, son of Ephraim, No. 32, b. in Bridgewater, Mass., 1748 ; m. Jane, daughter John Holman, 1771 ;
had a large family, and removed to Minot, Maine, where he d.
1828, aged 80 years.

His children were:

I. JANE, b. 1773, m. Zenas Keith, 1792.

II. SALOME, b. 1774. m. R. Kinsley, 1794.

III. CYRUS,* b. 1777.

IV. WILLIAM H., b. May 12, 1779. No. 133.

V. EPHRAIM, b. 1782. No. 134.

VI. SHEPHARD, b. 1784. d. at Dorchester, Mass., in infancy.

VII. SUSANNA, b. 1787. m. John Eaton, of Dorchester, Mass., 1812.

VIII. FRANCIS,† b. 1789.

IX. JASON, b. 1791. d. in infancy.

X. ASENATH, b. 1793. ·Went to Minot, Maine. d. unm.

XI. HARMONY, b. 1796. m. James Watson, 1821.

No. 69.

LEWIS CARY, son of Daniel, No. 33, b. in Morris county, N. J. 1742; lived on the paternal estate, and in 1777 bought two hundred acres of land near Drakesville, where he d. 1817. He was m. three times.

---

*CYRUS, m. Nabby Keith, 1802; removed west, and n. t. of family.
†FRANCIS, m. Harriet Haywood, 1816, E. Bridgewater. n. t. of family.

His children were:

  I.   DANIEL, b. 1770. d. in infancy.

  II.   JACOB b. July 7, 1772. d. unm. 1823.

  III. JANE, b. 1775. m. —— Drake. d. at Princeton,
        Illinois, 1854.

  IV.   JOSEPH, b. October 17, 1778. No. 135.

  V.   SALLY, b. 1780. m. —— Rhoades. d. Sussex
        county, N. J., 1807.

  VI.   ABEL, b. June 1781. No. 136.

  VII. LEWIS, b. October 19, 1783. No. 137.

  VIII. AARON, b. September 26, 1785. No. 138.

  IX.   JOHN, b. March 7, 1788. No. 139.

  X.   EZRA,* b. November 29, 1791.

  XI.   DANIEL, b. May 28, 1793. No. 140.

  XII. MARTHA, b. 1794. m. —— Gale. Lives in In-
        diana.

  XIII. NANCY,† ⎫
                  ⎬ b. 1796.
  XIV. LAURANA,‡ ⎭

  XV.   GEORGE L., b. May 29, 1799. No. 141.

  XVI. ANN ELIZA, b. 1801. m. D. P. Marchant, Mor-
        ris county, N. J.

---

*EZRA, m. and had one son, Lewis E. He d. 1844, and his son Lewis
E. d. unm. in 1846.

†NANCY, m. first, —— McCauley; and second, —— Mitchell, in Richland county, Ohio.

‡LAURANA, m. —— Merriam, Wyandotte county, Ohio.

No. 70.

AARON CARY, son of Ichabod, No. 34, b. in Bridgewater, Mass., April 6, 1751; removed to Colerain, Mass. ; m. Jemima Atwood, May 31, 1781. He d. in Colerain, September 30, 1830, aged 80 years. His wife. d. Feb. 19, 1837.

His children were :

I.   ZENAS, b. November 26, 1782.   No. 142.

II. SUSANNA, b. June 20, 1783.   m. —— Burns.   d. in Ohio.

III. —— a son, } TWINS } d. in infancy.
IV. —— a son, } b. Jan. 23, 1785. }

V.   HANNAH, b. November 5, 1787.   m. E. Prouty, of Heath, Mass.

VI. LEVI, b. May 12, 1790.   Killed at battle of Tippecanoe, Ind., 1811.

VII. CHARLOTTE, b. November 15, 1797.   d. August 31, 1803.

No. 71.

CAPT. HOVARD CARY, son of Col. Simeon, No. 35, b. in Bridgewater, Mass., 1760; m. Huldah, daughter of Samuel Packard, 1785. He was a Justice of the Peace ; a member of the Constitutional Convention, and the first Representative from North Bridgewater, in the Legislature.

His children were :

    I.   SIMEON,* b. 1786.

    II.   DANIEL HOWARD,† b. 1788.

    III.   ZENAS,‡ b. 1790.

    IV.   WILLIAM, b. 1792. m. —— Alden. n. t.

    V.   ELBRIDGE, b. 1794. d. in infancy.

    VI.   FRANCIS, b. 1796. m. —— Alden. n. t.

    VII.   MOLLY, b. 1798. m. Ezra Dunham.

    VIII.   RHODA, b. 1800. m. Major Nathan Haywood.

    IX.   ZIBA, b. 1802. d. in youth.

No. 72.

JOSIAH CARY, son of Zebulon, No. 36, b. in Bridgewater, Mass., 1754; removed when young to Brookfield, Mass., m. Molly Moulton, 1780; and had by her six children. She d. 1795, and he m. second, Lydia Hale, who bore him four children.

*SIMEON, m. Roana Howard, 1806, and moved to Maine. n. t. Dr. Nelson·H. Cary, of Wayne, Maine, was a son of Simeon. He is the father of the world renowned singer Anna Louisa.

†DANIEL H., m. Martha, daughter of Gideon Howard, 1812. n. t.

‡ZENAS, removed to Maine.

His children were :

   I.   ZEBULON, b. October 5, 1781. No. 143.

  II.   JOSIAH, b. April 7; 1783. No. 144.

 III.   POLLY, b. March 22, 1785. m. Samuel Horrs, 1805. d. April 25, 1808.

 IV.   PATTY, b. March 16, 1787. m. —— Cummings, d. December 26, 1846.

  V.   AVERY, b. February 17, 1789. No. 145.

 VI.   LUTHER,* b. December 20, 1793.

VII.   LYDIA, b. March 17, 1797. m. James Titus, 1834. d. July 29, 1852.

VIII.   JONATHAN, b. September 10, 1798. No. 146.

 IX.   MORDECAI,† b. October 5, 1799.

  X.   THOMAS, b. August 15, 1802. No. 147.

No. 73.

RECOMPENCE CARY, son of Zebulon, No. 36, b. in Bridgewater, January 25, 1757; went to Ward, Mass., was a mechanic; a soldier in the Revolutionary war; engaged in mercantile pursuits in Ward, (now Auburn), represented that

*LUTHER, m. three times; had one son Luther, who died in infancy, and a daughter Mary Anna, who m. Timothy M. Duncan; lived in North Brookfield, Mass., and d. September 12, 1869.

†MORDECAI, m. Betsy Bruce, 1832; had no children, and lives at West Brookfield, Mass.

town in the Legislature ; and was an official member of the Congregational church.   While on a visit to a daughter in Erie county, N. Y., he d. December 13, 1836, aged 80 years, leaving the rich legacy of a good name to his children. He m. Anna Drury, 1789.

His children were :

   I.   ZEBULON,* b. July 26, 1790.

   II. LEONARD, b. April 2, 1793.   No. 148.

  III. CLARISSA,† b. September 19, 1797.

  IV. ELIZA,‡ b. July 17, 1802.

No. 74.

MOSES CARY, son of Jonathan, No. 37, b. in Bridge-water, Mass., November 20, 1748 ; m. Susanna, daughter of Jabez Field, 1773.   In 1824 he published a pamphlet, containing a sketch of the families of North Bridgewater, which has aided in perfecting these memorials.   He d. December 1827, aged 81 years.

*ZEBULON, m. Martha Baird, but had no children ; he was a prominent, honored and useful man.   His widow lives in Macon Ga.

†CLARISSA, m. Rev. Isaac Oakes; lives in Livingston county, N. Y.. no children.

‡ELIZA, m. Rev. Dr. Cannon, of Geneva, N. Y., for twenty-eight years District Secretary of Am. B. F. M., and resides at Geneva ; has two daugh ters, both married.

His children were:

   I.   LUCIUS,* b. July 28, 1776.

   II.   BARILLIA, b. August 25, 1780. No. 149.

   III.   SUSANNA, b. April 27, 1783. m. Rev. John Shaw, 1807.

   IV.   POLLY, b. November 13, 1785. m. Jonathan Bealls. d. 1850.

   V.   CASSANDRA, b. February 1, 1768. d. unm. 1862.

No. 75.

JONATHAN CARY, son of Jonathan, No. 37, b. in Bridge-water, Mass., February 14, 1757; m. Abigail, a daughter of Jonathan Perkins, 1784. He was a Revolutionary soldier; drew a pension until his death, December 25, 1852, aged 95 years.

---

*LUCIUS, graduated at Brown University, R. I., in 1798; studied law; went to Charleston, S. C., and d. April, 1806.

His children were:

    I.   HULDAH, b. 1785. m. Darius Howard.

    II.   CALEB, b. 1788. No. 150.

    III.   JONATHAN, b. 1791. No. 151.

    IV.   LUTHER, b. 1794. No. 152.

    V.   MARTIN, b. 1795. No. 153.

    VI.   ABIGAIL, b. about 1797. m. Isaac Dunham.

    VII.   SALLY, b. about 1799. m. Zibo Keith.

    VIII.   MARY, b. about 1800. m. James Littlefield.

    IX.   AURELIA, b. about 1802. d. in infancy.

    X.   NANCY, b. 1804. d. in infancy.

No. 76.

ALPHEUS CARY, son of Jonathan, No. 37, b. in Bridge-water, Mass., April 21, 1761 ; m. Ruby Perkins, September 21, 1786 ; lived in Quincy, Mass., over thirty years, and d. in Milton, Mass., November 1, 1816. She d. in Boston, 1836

His children were:

I.   NANCY,* b. July 7, 1787.

II.   ALPHEUS, b. November 4, 1788. No. 154.

III.   LUCY,† b. April 3, 1790.

IV.   CHARLES, b. September 26, 1794. unm. in North Bridgewater.

V.   GEORGE, ⎫   TVINS,   ⎰ d. in infancy.

VI.   RUBY,   ⎬   b. 1795.   ⎱ d. in infancy.

VII.   GEORGE, b. September 25, 1796. d. in Boston. unm.

VIII.   LEVIS, b. March 31, 1798. No. 155.

IX.   RUBY, b. January 16, 1800. d. unm. in Haverhill, June 17, 1847.

X.   ISAAC, ⎫   TWINS   ⎰ No. 156.

XI.   ZIBA, ⎬ b. June 25, 1802. ⎱ d. unm. Nov. 10, 1831.

XII.   ABIGAIL,‡ b. March, 1806.

No. 77.

JAMES CARY, son of Jonathan, No. 37, b. in Bridgewater, Mass., April 22, 1766; m. Hannah, daughter of Samuel Alden, 1798, and had one daughter; his wife d. and he m. Hannah, daughter of Thomas Wales, 1803, and had three other children.

*NANCY, m. Lemuel Hall, and had one son and two daughters; she d. 1862.

†LUCY, m. Hazen Morse, November 6, 1814; and had eleven children; she d. July 28, 1860.

‡ABIGAIL, m. —— Frobisher, and had one son and one daughter; and d. April 27, 1829.

His children were:

    I.   Lydia, b. 1800. m. Ephraim Howard, 1821.

    II. Otis, b. June 14, 1804. No. 157.

    III. Nancy, b. 1807. m. Elbridge Packard.

    IV. Austin, b. 1809. No. 158.

No. 78.

Isaac Cary, son of John, No. 38, b. in Bridgewater, Mass., February 1, 1742; went when a child with his father to Mendham, Morris county, N. J., inherited one-half his father's farm, and moved to Sussex county, N. J. m. ――― and d. 1791. Very little information can be obtained as to family or their descendants.

His children were:

    I.   Abram, b. about 1762. No. 159.

    II. Isaac, b. about 1764.   n. t.

    III. Jacob, b. about 1766.   n. t.

    IV. Joseph, b. about 1768.   n. t.

    V. Martha, b. about 1770.   n. t.

    VI. Phebe, b. about 1772. m. ――― Bosley.

No. 79.

JOHN CARY, son of John, No. 38, b. in Morris county, N. J., July 25, 1757; m. Joanna Lyon, December 28, 1778, and lived and d. on the homestead of his father. He d. 1824.

His children were:

I. HENRY, b. January 6, 1780. No. 160.

II. CLEMENT, b. May 22, 1782. No. 161.

III. NATHANIEL, b. November 23, 1784. d. January 14, 1785.

IV. NATHANIEL, b. December 5, 1786. No. 162.

V. DAVID, b. February 25, 1789. d. May 5, 1793.

VI. MARY,* b. September 8, 1761.

VII. JOHN, b. September 3, 1794. d. February 20, 1797.

VIII. JOHN, b. May 27, 1797. No. 163.

IX. ISAAC, b. August 16, 1799. d. September 11, 1799.

X. ISAAC, b. November 18, 1800. No. 164.

---

*MARY, m. Rev. Ezra H. Day, 1814; moved to New Albany, Indiana; her husband d. 1823, and she m. Major Silas Miller; he d. 1855, and she returned to Norristown, N. J. She had three children by her first husband.

No. 80.

EBENEZER CARY, son of Michael, No. 43, b. in Barrington, Mass., m. about 1765 ; lived and d. in Barrington.

His children were :

   I.   NATHAN, b. 1814. n. t.

  II.   EBENEZER, b. 1816. No. 165.

No. 81.

CHAD. CARY, son of Thomas, No. 44, b. in Smithfield, R. I., May 17, 1773; was a farmer, m. Elizabeth Smith, of Providence, R. I., January 16, 1791 ; a woman of considerable talent, and author of several poems. He d. in North Killingly, Ct., September 5, 1839.

His children were :

I. ANNA,* b. January 9, 1792.

II. POLLY,† b. April 30, 1794.

III. EBENEZER, b. August 6, 1797. No. 166.

IV. WILLIAM, b. March 28, 1799. No. 167.

V. GEORGE S., b. September 6, 1801. No. 168.

VI. SUSAN T.,‡ b. August 17, 1803.

VII. ELIZABETH,‖ b. April 21, 1805.

VIII. SALLY S.,§ b. November 7, 1806.

IX. ABBY T.,(a) b. July 7, 1808.

X. EMELINE, b. November 7, 1809. unm. North Woodstock, Ct.

XI. ALMIRA, b. October 17, 1811. unm. North Woodstock, Ct.

XII. CHAD. B., b. April 17, 1813. No. 169.

XIII. JOHN H., b. May 1, 1816. No. 170,

*ANNA, m. January 1, 1816, to Amasa Olney, of Providence, R. I., had six children : d. in Weir, Mass.

†POLLY, m. Andrew Burlingame, farmer, of Situate, R. I., March 22, 1821 ; had six children ; when last heard from she resided at Putnam, Ct.

‡SUSAN T., m. May 15, 1835, to William Walker, of East Woodstock, Ct. Now living there; no child.

‖ELIZABETH, m. May 25, 1834, to Charles Hibbard, farmer, of North Woodstock, Conn. Now living there; two children.

§SALLY S., m. March 22, 1829, to Nodiah Flint, farmer, of Thompson, Ct., has two children.

(a)ABBY T., m. October 17, 1831, to Leonard Thompson, merchant, of Columbia, Ct., had two children, viz : Dr. Bradford Thompson, Physician and Surgeon in regular army during the rebellion, now practicing in New York City; and second, Elizabeth, who m. October 28, 1863, to Sewell Green, a retired gentlemen in New York City. Abby T., the mother, lives in New York City.

No. 82.

JOSEPH CARY, son of Joseph, No. 45, b. in Mansfield, Ct., March 7, 1757; m. Rachel Thompson, in Canterbury, Ct., January 7, 1781; removed to Middlefield, Mass., and later to Ontario county, N. Y., where he d. February 3, 1848. His wife d. September 26, 1851.

His children were:

I. RACHEL,* b. March 31, 1782

II. JOSEPH, b. January 19, 1784. No. 171.

III. LUCY,† b. December 1, 1785.

IV. STEPHEN,‡ b. October 6, 1787.

V. EZEKIEL, b. April 1, 1789. n. t.

VI. HANNAH,|| b. January 3, 1792.

VII. EUNICE,§ b. January 15, 1795.

VIII. PHEBE,(a) b. September 15, 1797.

IX. ZINA,(b) b. February 1, 1799.

X. ISAAC, b. September 15, 1804. No. 172.

*RACHEL, m. Ethan Billens, of Conway, Mass., and had four children; she was living in 1865.

†LUCY, m. William Mott, in Middlefield, Mass., and had one son and four daughters.

‡STEPHEN, m. and had one son and two daughters; and d. at New Orleans in 1814.

||HANNAH, m. —— Scott, and had five children.

§EUNICE, m. —— Wright.

(a)PHEBE, m. —— Frazer, and had five children.

(b)ZINA, m. —— Gill, and had four children.

No. 83.

RICHARD CARY, son of Joseph, No. 45, b. in Mansfield, Ct., January 15, 1759; m. Susanna Ford, 1782, in Williamsburg, Mass., removed to Nelson, Madison county, N. Y., in 1806. He was a soldier seven years in the Revolutionary war; he d. December, 1841.

His children were:

    I.   SUSANNA,* b. 1784.

    II. LUCY,† b. 1786·

   III. PHEBE,‡ b. 1788.

  IV. CLARISSA,‖ b. 1790.

    V. CALVIN,§ b. June, 1792.

  VI. RICHARD M., b. December 11, 1794. No. 173.

 VII. LUTHER H., b. February, 1800. No. 174.

VIII. RELIEF, b. 1802. m. William Titus, 1821. d. 1838.

*SUSANNA, m. C. Doolittle, 1803; d. in Illinois, 1858.

†LUCY, m. Nathan Streeter, 1804; d. in Erie county, N. Y., 1809.

‡PHEBE, m. Jonathan Burns; d. in Erie county, N. Y., 1843.

‖CLARISSA, m. Talcut Patchin, an officer of the U. S. army, who was wounded at the battle of Chippewa, in the war of 1812. She was living in Erie county, N. Y., in 1865.

§CALVIN, was killed in a hand to hand fight with three indians, at the burning of Buffalo, in 1813; he was a man of giant frame, weighing three hundred pounds, fine proportion, herculean in strength, and a swift runner.

No. 84.

ABNER CARY, son of Joseph, No. 45, b. in Williamsburg, Mass., January 31, 1760 ; m. four times in Williamsburg, had six children born there, and removed to Dupage county, Illinois, where he d. 1845, aged 85 years.

His children were :

    I.   LUCINA,* b. February 22, 1793.

    II. ABNER L., b. at Junction, Illinois. n. t.

    III. ALVIN.   n. t.

    IV. LUCY.   n. t.

    V.   SALLY.   n. t.

    VI. ASA.   n. t.

No. 85.

ASA CARY, son of Joseph No. 45, b. in Williamsburg, Mass., April 1, 1770 ; m. Damaris Hickox, in Conway, Mass., June 24, 1790 ; removed to Erie county, N. Y., where he d. Sept. 19, 1852.   His widow d. April 17, 1863, aged 91 years.

*LUCINA, m. William W. Leonard, in Middlefield, Mass.

His children were:

   I.   TRUMAN, b. May 31, 1791. No. 175.

   II.   SYLVIA,* b. June 17, 1793.

   III.   ASA, b. July 18, 1795. d. June 19, 1808.

   IV.   JOSEPH, b. December 24, 1797. No. 176.

   V.   SYLVESTER, b. May 5, 1800. No. 177.

   VI.   HARRIET,† b. January 13, 1803.

   VII.   VAN RANSALEER, b. January 5, 1805. No. 178.

   VIII.   DAMARIS,‡ b. March 31, 1807.

   IX.   AURILLA,‖ b. October 11, 1809.

   X.   SADUSKA,§ b. January 6, 1812.

   XI.   ALMIRA,(a) b. August 8, 1814.

   XII.   ASA, b. August 22, 1821. No. 179.

No. 86.

EBENEZER CARY, son of Ebenezer, No. 48, b. in Mansfield, Ct., December 27, 1758; was a revolutionary soldier; he went with Joseph Elliott, as a surveyor, in 1798, for the Holland Land Company, to Western New York; when over

*SYLVIA, m. Aaron Adams, of Boston, N. Y., December 24, 1809; had five sons and one daughter; and is living at Boston, N. Y.

†HARRIET, m. Erastus Torrey, October 8, 1821, in Boston, N. Y., had six children; d. July 30, 1850, at Silver Creek, Illinois.

‡DAMARIS, m. Perry J. Jencks, September 9, 1823; had eight children; resides in Wapau, Wisconsin.

‖AURILLA, m. Hiram Memmenway, September 6, 1827; had three children; and d. at Freeport, Illinois, March 30, 1858.

§SADUSKA, m. Tillinghast Vaughn; had six children; lives in Louisana,

(a)ALMIRA, m. September 10, 1832, to Rev. George Wilkinson; had five children; she d. at Painted Post, N. Y., January 22, 1848.

sixty years of age he m. Elizabeth Cunningham, a widow;
and d. May 16, 1825.

His children were:

    I.   SARAH,* b. about 1812.

    II. LUCINDA, b. 1814. d. unm. January 5, 1849.

    III. EBENEZER, b. 1816. No. 180.

No. 87.

TRUMBULL CARY, son of Ebenezer, No. 48, b. in Mansfield, Ct., August 11, 1787; removed to Western New York,
m. Margaret E. Brisbane, at Batavia, N. Y., June 2, 1812.
He served as Adjutant in the war of 1812; rendered honorable service in both branches of the Legislature of New York;
was appointed by Governor Seward, Bank Commissioner, in
1838, which position he held for three years. He d. June 20,
1869; his wife d. June 22, 1863. He had four children, three
of whom d. in infancy. He left one son.

His children were:

    I.   WALTER, b. 1818. No. 181.

    II. ELIZABETH, b. February 24, 1822. d. February
        8, 1823.

    III. ELIZABETH ANN, b. June 13, 1824. d. June 24,
        1824.

    IV. TRUMBULL, b. October 4, 1829. d. April 1, 1832.

*SARAH, m. John D. Verplank, and had children; she d. at Brooklyn.
N. Y., 1859.

No. 88.

EZEKIEL CARY, son of Deacon John, No. 49, b. in Scotland, December 7, 1741; lived and d. in the part of Windham, which is now called Willimantic; was a tanner and shoemaker by trade. He married Zervia, daughter of Deacon Nathaniel Skiff, March 15, 1764; he d. May 14, 1872; his widow d. July 18, 1816, aged 82 years.

His children were:

I. JOHN,* b. June 7, 1766.

II. DIANTHA,† b. July 14, 1768.

III. WALDO, b. April 3, 1772. No. 182.

No. 89.

WILLIAM CARY, son of Deacon John, No. 49. b. in Scotland, Ct., October 25, 1747; m. first, Irena, daughter of Josiah Manning, May 16, 1771, by whom he had eight children ; she d. November 17, 1795. aged 48, and he m. second, Celia (Darby) Bushnell, widow of Ezekiel Bushnell, of Lisbon, Ct., March, 1801. He d. July 20, 1812; his widow d. October 12, 1844, aged 89 years.

*JOHN, was a shoemaker; removed to Baltimore, Md., where he d. unm. in middle life.

†DIANTHA, m. Andrew Baker; had no children and d. in old age of cancer.

His children were :

    I. ALATHEA, b. December 1773. d. unm. November, 1795.

    II. CHLOE, b. January 20, 1776. d. unm. November, 1795.

  III. JOHN, b. March 18, 1778. No. 183.

  IV. ELIJAH, b. October 4, 1780. No. 184.

   V. WILLIAM, b. December 11, 1782. No. 185.

  VI. THERON. b. 1786. d. December 7, 1809. unm.

 VII. NATHANIEL, b. 1789. d. November 29, 1834. unm.

VIII. PHEBE, b. 1791. d. November, 1795.

No. 90.

JONATHAN CARY, son of Deacon John, No. 49, b. in Scotland, Ct., June 5, 1849; he m. Martha, daughter of Elisha Hurlbut, September 21, 1775, and in 1791 removed to Norwich, Ct., where he d.

His children were :

I.   IRENA, b. August 17, 1777.   m. Capt. Elias Lord, of Norwich.

II. THOMAS, b. July 8, 1779.   d. at sea.   unm.

III. ALFRED, b. June 29, 1781.   d. at sea.   unm.

IV. FREDERICK, b. February 14. 1786.   No. 186.

V.   RALPH, b. June 2, 1789.   No. 187.

VI. FANNY, b. July 26, 1791.   m. Capt. James Snow, of New York.

VII. WINTHROP, b. 1793.   d. at sea.   m.

No. 91.

CAPT. JAMES CARY, son of Beneijah, No. 50, b. in Scotland, Ct., November 27, 1750; was a prominent and wealthy farmer in Scotland, and served with distinction in the war of Independence. His estate after his death was valued at $80,000. He m. first, Abigail, daughter of Joseph Kingsley, of Pomfret, Ct., August 12, 1773; she d. December 18, 1807. He m. second, Anna (Spaulding) Bradford, widow of Rev. William Bradford, 1809. He d. February 28, 1827.

His children were:

I.   ABIGAIL,* b. January 28, 1775.

II.   JAMES, b. December 9, 1777.   No. 188.

III.   BENEIJAH, b. January 4, 1780.   d. unm. August
       24, 1808.

IV.   ANNA, b. February 21, 1782.   d. March 3, 1781.

V.   SANFORD, b. July 14, 1784.   No. 189.

VI.   SALLY, b. September 7, 1786.   m. Thomas Morse,
      of Woodstock, Ct.

No. 92.

ROGER CARY, son of Capt. Nathaniel Cary, No. 51. b.
in Scotland, Ct., January 7, 1759; was a trader and speculator,
and d. at the South.   He m. Eunice Parish, January 27, 1780.

His children were:

I.   NATHANIEL, b. September 16, 1780.   n. t.

II.   JOSEPH, b. July 4, 1783.   n. t.

III.   EUNICE,† b. December 3, 1787.

---

*ABIGAIL, m. Parker Morse, October 6, 1798, by whom she had five
children; when last heard from she was living in Canterbury, Ct., at the
age of 90.

†EUNICE, m. —— Storer, and settled at Cherry Valley, N. Y.

No. 93.

ANSON CARY, son of Capt. Nathaniel, No. 51, b. in Scotland, Ct., March 15, 1762; m. Hannah Carew. of Norwich, Ct., was an early settler in Chenango county, New York, at Oxford, where he resided until he d. May 8, 1842, aged 80 years. He was a blacksmith by trade, a man of unusually large and muscular frame, of great strength physically and mentally. He was a Justice of the Peace twenty years; Sheriff of the County for four years, and several years a Judge of the Court. He was a very prominent, influential and useful citizen.

His children were:

I.   HORATIO, b. March 27, 1785.   No. 190.

II.   MINERVA,* b. October 17, 1787.

III.   HARRIET,† b. July 29, 1789.

IV.   GEORGE A., b. May 8, 1793.   No. 191.

V.   PALMER C., b. March 31, 1798.   No. 192.

VI.   ZALMON·S., b. August 31, 1800.   No. 193.

VII.   HANNAH, b. June 17, 1802.

VIII. ALBERT G.,‡ b. July 20, 1807.

*MINERVA, m. Amos A. Franklin, and removed to Grant county, Wisconsin; had seven children, and d. May 25, 1859.

†HARRIET, m. A. B. Bennett, and had two sons; she d. August 9, 1863.

‡ALBERT G., m. Melissa Madison, by whom he had three children, all of whom died childless. Albert G. when last heard from was living at Oxford, Chenango county, N. Y.

No. 94.

CHRISTOPHER CARY, son of Dr. Samuel, No. 52, b. in
Windham, Ct.; went when a boy with his father to Lyme,
N. H., then almost a wilderness.   He joined the army of the
Revolution at a very early age; served under Colonel Waite,
of New Hampshire; was twice taken prisoner, and suffered
incredible hardships.   He removed to Ohio in 1802, and
settled in Cincinnati.   He was pre-eminently a child of mis-
fortune during his whole life.   When very young he accidentally lost one eye; a few years later he was made a cripple for
life, by being caught under a falling tree.   He was always
roving, never contented in any situation.   He traveled east,
west, north and south, often spending months among the indians; he was robbed, shipwrecked, and subjected to all
kinds of hardships and misfortunes.   An accurate history of
his life would be more thrilling than a work of fiction.   He
had a stout frame and an iron constitution; he d. near Cincinnati, O., February, 1837.   He was three times m. viz:
first, to Elsie Terrel, in Lyme, N. H., in 1784; second, Lear
Brokaw, in Cincinnati; and third, to Margaret McCarty, in
1825.   He was a revolutionary pensioner at the time of his
death.

His children were:

I. Lucy,* b. 1784.

II. Robert, b. January 24, 1787. No. 194.

III. Beneijah, b. 1788. No. 195.

IV. Maria, b. 1790. m. John Loring, 1808.

V. Christopher, b. 1792. Killed accidentally in Cincinnati, 1807.

VI. Irvin, b. 1826. No. 196.

VII. Maria, b. 1828. d. in childbed.

VIII. Anna, b. 1831. m. —— Sprong, and d. in Missouri, 1864.

No. 95.

John Cary, son of Dr. Samuel, No. 52, b. at Lyme, N. H., December 26, 1780; removed to the State of New York; settled at Hudson, where he resided many years; then removed to Onondago county, New York; and thence to Ohio some years before his death; he d. at Ashtabula, O., March 23, 1863, aged 82 years. He m. first, Harriet Knapp, of Hudson, N. Y., 1806, and late in life m. a second wife, whom he survived.

*Lucy, m. James McGinnis, Cincinnati, O.; had several children, one of whom is Mrs. William McCammon, Esq., of Cincinnati; she d. at advanced age.

His children were:

    I.   ORRIN, b. July 16, 1807. No. 197.

    II. HARRIET,* b. 1809.

    III. FRANKLIN,† b. 1811.

    IV. LORENZO, b. 1813. No. 198.

    V. DELIA,‡ b. 1815.

    VI. JOHN, b. 1817. Living in Chicago, Illinois. unm.

No. 96.

WILLIAM CARY, son of Dr. Samuel, No. 52, b. in Lyme, N. H., January 28, 1783; emigrated to the Northwest Territory with mother and brother Christopher, settling in Cincinnati in 1802; bought a small farm at the head of Main street, where he resided until 1814, when he sold his thirty.two acres in Cincinnati, and settled on Section 30, Millcreek Township, (now College Hill); vhere he resided until his death, March 25, 1862. He represented Hamilton County in the Legislature, in 1824–5; and was an active supporter of the Canal Bill, and the First Free School Law of Ohio. He was remarkable for his amiability of disposition,

---

*HARRIET, m. —— Lockwood; lived in Ashtabula, O.; had a large family and d. 1863.

†FRANKLIN, never m. Went to Louisiana before the late war, and has not been heard from since.

‡DELIA, m. Dr. Jonathan W. Brooks, of Norwich, Ct., and had large family, and lives now in Chicago.

purity of character, public spirit and benevolence. He was many years an elder in the Presbyterian Church, and a frequent representative to the General Assembly. He originated the churches at Mount Pleasant and College Hill; endowed a professorship in Farmer's College, and was a patron of all the benevolent enterprises of the day. He d. in the full assurance of a blessed immortality. He m. Rebecca, a daughter of Roswell and Deborah Fenton, January 8, 1809, who still survives, aged 83 years.

His children were :

I. FREEMAN GRANT, b. April 7, 1810. No. 199.

II. WILLIAM WOODVARD, b. February 23, 1812. No. 200.

III. SAMUEL FENTON, b. February 18, 1814. No. 201.

No. 97.

JOSIAH CARY, son of Josiah, No. 53, b. in Haddam Ct., January 16, 1761 ; m. Lydia Clark, 1783 ; he lived in Middle Haddam, and followed the coasting trade ; he d. April 14, 1797.

His children were:

    I. CHARLOTTE b. May 30, 1784. m. —— Loomis.

   II. NANCY, b. August 31, 1787. m. —— Anable.

 III. JOSIAH, b. January 23, 1791. No. 202.

 IV. HANNAH, b. June 19, 1793. m. —— Bumphrey.

   V. LYDIA, b. June 26, 1795. m. —— Skinner.

Sixth Generation.

No. 98.

Henry Lucius Cary, son of Eleazer, No. 54, b. in Windham, Ct., October 18, 1769; m. Mary Harris, September 7, 1812, and d. May 3, 1848, leaving one son.

His children were:

    I.   Lucius Henry, who m. in Norwich, Ct., and has one child.

No. 99.

ELEAZER CARY, son of Nathaniel, No. 55, b. in Windham, Ct., December 14, 1769; was a goldsmith, resided in Windham most of his life, thence removed to Norwich, Ct. He was quite a musician, and especially skilled in playing the violin; he was widely known as "Eleazer the Fiddler." He m. Matilda, daughter of John Parrish, November 23, 1791; he d. November 8, 1820; his widow d. at Willimantic, Ct., November 10, 1845.

His children were:

I. THOMAS STORRS, b. March 21, 1792. d. unm. March, 1823.

II. LUCIA, b. January 2, 1794. d. February 27, 1795.

III. LUCIA,* b. June 16, 1795

IV. HARRIET,† b. December 29, 1799

V. LYDIA,‡ b. 1803.

VI. ELEAZER, b. 1811. No. 203.

*LUCIA, m. first, Samuel Welch, and had three children; m. second, William Russel, and had three children; and is a widow in Buffalo, N. Y.

†HARRIET, m. Oliver Lathrop, had two children; resides in Willimantic, Ct.

‡LYDIA, m. first, Mr. Ware, of Hartford, Ct., and had two children; m. second, m. —— Gardner, and had one child, and resides in Marydosia, Morgan county, Illinois.

No. 100.

Olivet S. Cary, son of Olivet, No. 57, b. in Lempster, N. H., November 6, 1810; m. Mehitabel Keyes, of Acworth, December 27, 1837, where he still resides.

His children were:

I. Chester E., b. March 11, 1839. Printer in Montpelier, Vt.

II. Georgiana, b. November 20, 1841. m. September 11, 1862, Dr. S. M. Dinsmore, of Antrim, N. H.

III. Frank Pierce, b. 1848, resides in Terre Haute, Indiana.

No. 101.

Alden Cary, son of Elliott Cary, No. 58, b. in Lempter, N. H., 1801; settled on the paternal estate in Lempster, where he resided when last heard from. He m. Hannah B. Wellman, 1824.

His children were :

I. ANGELINE, b. 1826.   m. Orson Gee, 1848.
II. CARLOS, b. 1828.   d. 1838.
III. WILSON,* b. 1831.
IV. RUFUS,† b. 1833.
V. FRANCIS,‡ b. 1836.
VI. HANNAH, b. 1838.   m. Charles Giffin, 1859.

No. 102.

WILLIAM CARY, son of William, No. 59, b. in Lempster, N. H., February 12, 1796; m. Sophia Hurd, May 22, 1817; removed with his family to Amesbury, Mass; he d. at Malden, Mass., May 8, 1857.

*WILSON, is a machinist and lives in Lowell, Mass.   m. 1854.
†RUFUS, m. 1856, and is in the boot and shoe business, Acworth, N. H.
‡FRANCIS, m. 1863; is a farmer, and resides in Lempster, N. H.

His children were:

I.   WILLIAM ADDISON, b. July 23, 1818. No. 204.

II. CALTHEA GILMORE, b. November 26, 1819. m. Francis C. Swett.

III. SOPHIA AUGUSTA, b. September 15, 1821. d. August 27, 1840. unm.

IV. MILAN GALUSHA, b. November 20, 1823. No. 205.

V.   AUGUSTUS CELAND,^us b. September 16, 1825. No. 206.

VI. HENRY GROSVENOR,* b. December 4, 1829.

No. 103.

BYFIELD CARY, son of William, No. 59, b. in Lempster, N. H., November 25, 1799; m. Hannah Mayo, in Acworth, N. H., November 20, 1823; removed to Ware, Mass., 1825, where he d. 1826. His widow m. —— Ormsby, and lives in Alsted, N. H.

His children were:

I.   EMELINE, b. 1824. m. —— Atwood, and lives in Alsted, N. H.; has four children.

*HENRY GROSVENOR, m. Mary K. Bagley; lives at ~~Amesbury,~~ Mass. No issue.   *malden*

No. 104.

Harvey Cary, son of William, No. 59, b. in Lempster, N. H., May 10, 1802; m. in Acworth, N. H., May 12, 1825, to Mary Barnard had two children born in Acworth, and removed about 1850 to Iowa, where he now resides.

His children were:

 I. Lucy Ann, b. July 5, 1828. m. and lives in Wisconsin.

 II. Lucia Emily, b. July 15, 1836. m. Wm. Hibb. Lives in Iowa, and has three children.

No. 105.

John M. Cary, son of William, No. 59, b. in Lempster, N. H., June 12, 1810; m. Susan Dart, of Guilford, Vt., October 17, 1832, and moved to Amesbury, Mass.

His children were:

 I. Ellen,* b. October 4, 1834

 II. William Henry, b. April 1, 1846. d. August 27, 1858.

The name of Cary became extinct in this branch.

*Ellen, m. Cyrus Shephard, of Amesbury, Mass.; had one child born at Alsted, N. H., February 25, 1858, at which date the mother d. and the child lives with grandmother at Amesbury.

No. 106.

Samuel Cary, son of Joseph, No. 61, b. in Providence, R. I., August 18, 1766; m. Elizabeth Cornwall, of Beekman, Duchess county, N. Y., September 25, 1791; and settled at Rensalaerville, Albany county, whence they removed to the City of Albany, 1827, where they resided until 1830, when they removed to Bethlehem, N. Y. Samuel in early life joined the Society of Friends, and both himself and his wife Elizabeth, were most acceptable preachers, and were in the habit of attending and preaching at many "Yearly Meetings." They lived blameless and eminently useful lives, adorning the doctrines they professed. The savour of their good names, and the influence of their example and precept are yet widely felt and acknowledged. After their demise their memoirs were published and widely circulated. He d. February 16, 1845, aged 79; his wife d. March 8, 1842. As their lives were exemplary, their deaths were peaceful and triumphant.

His children were:

I. RUTH, b. January 10, 1793. d. January 19, 1793.

II. ALBERT, b. February 23, 1794. d. May 16, 1831.

III. ABEL, b. November 12, 1795. d. May 16, 1798.

IV. DEBORAH, b. November 18, 1797. d. October, 1798.

V. RHODA, b. September 6, 1799. m. Isaac Page, 1821. d. March 22, 1848.

VI. JOSEPH, b. January 30, 1802. No. 207.

VII. MARY, b. March 20, 1804. d. April, 1806.

VIII. DAVID H.,* b. November 7, 1806.

IX. MARIA,† b. May 24, 1809.

X. SAMUEL,‡ ⎫ TRIPLETS, ⎧
XI. ISAAC H., ⎬ b. May 7, 1812. ⎨ No. 208.
XII. ——— ⎭ ⎩ Still born.

XIII. GEORGE, b. November 30, 1814. No. 209.

No. 107.

JOSEPH CARY, son of Joseph, No. 61, b. in Plainfield, Ct., August 18, 1773; m. Ruby Ann Eaton, of Killingly, Ct., and settled in Coventry, R. I. He was an eminent physician, and was proprietor of a celebrated "family pill." He d. May 15, 1815.

*DAVID H., m. Miss Hyde, 1833; lives in Albany; no issue.
†MARIA, m. Isaac B. Briggs, November 11, 1832.
‡SAMUEL, m. Jane March, of Chester county, Pennsylvania, 1840; lives in Albany; no issue.

His children were:

I. CYNTHIA, b. February 12, 1798. m. Samuel
    Mowry, and d. January 11, 1823.

II. ALBIGENE WALDO, b. May 23, 1801.

III. JEREMIAH E., b. April 30, 1803. . No. 210.

IV. AURELIUS A.,* b. May 20, 1806.

V. BETSEY MATILDA, b. July 31, 1809. m. Daniel
    Horton, of Adrian, Michigan.

VI. ALFRED X., b. March 28, 1811. No. 211.

No. 108.

DARIUS H. CARY, son of Joseph, No. 61, b. in Plainfield,
Ct., March 24, 1777; removed to Richfield, N. Y., m. Patty
Whitney, 1803. d. February 8, 1863.

*AURELIUS A., settled in Granville, Washington county, N. Y., but un-
able to procure copy of records.

His children were:

 I. EMELINE, b. 1803. d. 1805.

 II. EMELINE, b. 1806. m. Benjamin P. Jones, 1830.

 III. JOSIAH WHITNEY, b. 1808. No. 212.

 IV. SON,   }   TWINS,
 V. DAUGHTER, }   b. 1810. } d. in infancy.

 VI. THEODORE, b. 1812. d. 1827.

 VII. SUSAN E., b. 1815. m. Isaac Gage, 1849.

 VIII. EDWIN, b. 1817. No. 213.

 IX. LAURA, b. 1820. unm. d. August 12, 1867.

 X. LUCY M., b. 1823. m. —— Judd, Cherry Valley, N. Y., 1846.

No. 109.

WILLIAM CARY, son of Joseph, No. 61, b. in Plainfield, Ct., April 12, 1779; removed to State of New York; m. Lydia Trask, at Paris, Oneida county, 1805. He d. at Mohawk, N. Y., 1854.

His children were:

   I.   JOSEPH, b. 1807. No. 214.

   II.   HANNAH T.,* b. 1809.

   III.   ALFRED,† b. 1813.

   IV.   HARRIET A., b. 1815.

   V.   WILLIAM H., b. 1816. No. 215.

   VI.   GEORGE W., b. 1819. No. 216.

   VII.   CHARLES JEROME,‡ b. 1821.

No. 110.

EZRA CARY, son of Joseph, No. 61, b. at Plainfield, Ct., August 25, 1785; m. and removed to Richfield, N. Y., where he d.

His children were:

   I.   EZRA. n. t.

   II.   ELIZA, m. —— William H. Hannah. n. t.

   III.   ZENEAH, m. —— Eddy. n. t.

   IV.   ABIGAIL. n. t.

   V.   ALBERT, of Norwich, N. Y. n. t.

   VI.   ALANSON, of Troy, N. Y. n. t.

---

*HANNAH T., m. first, A. Burpee, 1837; and second, R. Brownell, 1855.

†ALFRED, m. Zilpha Snow, 1833; and lives at Fort Plain, New York. No issue.

CHARLES JEROME, m. Elizabeth Gardener, 1857; she d. in 1857; he lives in Milwaukee, Wisconsin. No issue.

No. 111.

WILLIAM CARY, son of Ebenezer Cary, No. 62, b. in Beekman, Duchess county, N. Y., November 22, 1769; studied medicine; settled at "Half Moon," Saratoga county, N. Y., was distinguished as a man, and as a physician; he was a worthy and exemplary preacher in the Society of Friends, more than thirty years. He was three times m. first, Ruth Sweet, January 7, 1793; second, Harriet Cook, May 29, 1811; third, Kezia Jackson, November 17, 1826. He d. November 23, 1845.

His children were:

I.   MATILDA, b. July 23, 1794. m. Thomas M. South-wick, June 23, 1814.

II.   SETH, b. March 3, 1796. d. November 21, 1796.

III.   EBENEZER, b. November 5, 1797. No. 217.

IV.   LUCIUS, b. May 9, 1799. No. 218.

V.   JARVIS, b. May 23, 1801. No. 219.

VI.   JOHN MILTON, b. September 6, 1803. d. unm. at Albany, November 10, 1858.

VII.   MARIA, b. October 12, 1805. m. Henry Fowler, July 15, 1824.

VIII. CATHERINE, b. October 28, 1806. m. David De-
val, May 6, 1824.

IX. LYDIA, b. October 1, 1808. d. unm. Feb. 17, 1828.

X. WILLIAM,* b. August 23, 1813.

XI. RUTH, b. June 1, 1816. m. Andrew Holmes,
March 10, 1857.

XII. ISAAC, b. January 15, 1818. No. 220.

XIII. CHARLES J., b. October 19, 1827. d. July 9, 1853.

No. 112.

TAYLOR CARY, son of Ebenezer, No. 62, b. in Duchess
county, N. Y., March 3, 1773; m. Betty Langdon, 1794, and
settled in Clinton, Saratoga county, N. Y., for a time, as a
weaver, thence removed to Vernon, Oneida county, on a
farm. He d. at Lysander, N. Y., October 26, 1853.

*WILLIAM, lives at Crescent, Saratoga county, N. Y.; was a member of
the Legislature in 1852; have no record of his family.

His children were :

I.   JOHN, b. 1796. d. 1799.

II. LUCY, b. May 9, 1798. d. unm. at Vernon, N. Y.; 1817.

III. MARIA,* b. January 18, 1801.

IV. WILLIAM, b. July. 12, 1803. No. 221.

V.   HEPZIBAH, b. 1805. d. in infancy.

VI. LOUISA,† b. January 7, 1808.

VII. JOHN, b. March 20, 1810. No. 222.

VIII. ELECTA J., b. February 8, 1814. m. Samuel Alden, Lysander, N. Y., 1835.

IX. ELIZABETH, b. April 2, 1817. m. Anson Smith, Vernon, N. Y., February 17, 1835.

No. 113.

EGBERT CARY, son of Ebenezer, No. 62, b. in Duchess county, N. Y., April 12, 1789; m. Tamar Flaglin, 1813; settled on the homestead ; was a physician, and was a member of the Legislature of N. Y., 1827; he d. 1862.

*MARIA, m. Elias Cox, April 7, 1825; had four children, and resides in Lysander, Onondago county, N. Y.

†LOUISA, m. Ira Mattison, January, 1825; removed to Worthington, O., where she d. without issue, April 14, 1838.

His children were:

 I. SOPHIA, b. 1814. m. George Wilkinson, Pokeep-
   sie, N. Y.

 II. PHEBE, b. 1815. m. H. D. Platt, District of
   Columbia.

 III. CECILIA, b. 1818. m. Thomas J. Doughty, Eden,
   Wisconsin.

 IV. MATILDA, b. 1820. m. William S. Coggshall,
   Brooklyn, N. Y.

 V. EBENEZER, b. 1822. No. 223.

 VI. PHILIP F., b. 1826. n. t.

 VII. TAMAR, b. 1829. unm.

 VIII. DEVIT CLINTON, b. 1833. m. and lives in Washington, District of Columbia.

No. 114.

STURGIS CARY, son of Ebenezer, No. 62, b. in Duchess
county, N. Y., July 25, 1794; m. first, Sarah Flagler, December 17, 1818; she d. April 11, 1836, and he m. second,
Hannah A. Gray, (widow), February 27, 1841; he settled in
Binghampton, Broome county, N. Y., where he still resides.

His children were:

I.   SOLOMON FLAGLER, b. October 9, 1820.   No. 224.

II.   CORNELIA F., b. June 5, 1822.   m. T. R. Morgan, 1839.

III. CYNTHIA A., b. February 12, 1824.   d. unm. 1851.

IV.   OLIVER A., b. June 5, 1827.   No. 225.

V.   PHEBE M., b. May 10, 1829.   d. 1851.

VI.   JAMES STURGIS, b. June 12, 1833.   m. and lives at Binghampton, N. Y.

VII. ABEL DEFOREST, b. December 22, 1842.   d. in childhood.

VIII. ABIGAIL, b. 1844.   d. in childhood.

IX.   ANDREV S., b. March 6, 1846.

X.   CHARLES H., b. November 12, 1848.

XI.   ANNA M., b. May 16, 1853. •

No. 115.

JOHNSON CARY, son of Nathan, No. 63, b. in Wyoming Valley, 1783; removed with his father to Steuben county, N. Y., 1799; m. Susan Bassett, August 26, 1807; was a farmer and inn keeper; a quiet and very highly esteemed citizen; he d. at Arkport, N. Y., 1862.

His children were :

I.   JANE,* b. May 21, 1807.

II.   MARY ANN,† b. June 22, 1813.

III.   ELIZABETH,‡ b. June 5, 1815.

IV.   SUSAN,|| b. July 16, 1822.

V.   CAROLINE,§ ·b. July 1, 1824.

There being no son, the name of Cary became extinct in this branch of the family.

No. 116.

ELEAZER CARY, son of Nathan, No. 63, b. in Wyoming Valley, Pa., 1785 ; m. Fanny Slocum ; lived in Wilkesbarre, Pa., as a merchant; d. January 22, 1853.

His children were:

I.   FRANCIS,   n. t.

II.   RHODA.   n. t.

III.   DOUGLASS,   n. t.

*JANE, m. Lewis W. Dèy, and d. 1835, without issue.·

†MARY ANN, m. William H. Hurlbut, June 26, 1839; had two sons William and Avery,.and lives in Elgin, Illinois.

‡ELIZABETH, m. Calvin J. Reynolds, M. D., March, 1836; lives at Cuba, N. Y.; has two daughters, viz: Caroline, m. to Malcolm Nash, of Cuba, and Mary m. Rufus Hufstader, of Hornellsville, N. Y.

||SUSAN, m. Wm. T. Hurlbut, October 13, 1849, and lives in Arkport, N. Y.; has three children, Martha E., Caroline P., and Charles Henry. .

§CAROLINE, m. William S. Babbitt, M. D., December 15, 1847; settled in Olean, N. Y., April 24, 1859; had two children, Clarence and Caroline.

No. 117.

WILLIAM CARY, son of Nathan, No. 63, b. in Wyoming Valley, Pa., about 1787 ; m. Peniah Rodman, and lived near Wilkesbarre, Pa., where he d. 1825.

His children were :

   I.   ELEAZER.*

   II.   RUTH.†

   III.   JANE. n. t.

   IV.   MARIA.‡

No. 118.

CHRISTOPHER CARY, son of Nathan, No. 63, b. in Wyoming Valley, Pa., about 1791 ; m. Mary Sylvester, and lived highly respected and honored ; he d. January 1, 1844.

*ELEAZER is an eminent Physician, in Perry, Pike county, Illinois.

†RUTH, m. first, Calvin Stearns, and second, Jesse Gibbs, of West Almond, Allegany county, N. Y.; has no children.

‡MARIA, m. Rev. Robert R. Rook, and had two children, Bell and Eleazer.

His children were:

I.   CHARLES* S., b. November 15, 1829.

II.   RUTH, b. 1831. d. at 16 years of age.

III. JOHNSON,† b. July 2, 1833.

IV. MARY JANE,‡ b. November 1, 1835.

V.   HUBBARD, b. October 1, 1837.

VI. JOHN, b. June 1, 1840. d. at 21 years of age.

No. 119.

CEPHUS CARY, son of Ezra, No. 64, b. in New Jersey, 1775; accompanied his father when a child to Western Pennsylvania, and thence to Ohio in 1790, stopping for a time on the Ohio near Weeeling, Virginia, and thence to the wilderness in Shelby county, where he lived (at Sidney), until his death at the age of 94 years. He was three times m. first, to Jane Williamson, by whom he had nine children; second, Rhoda Jerard, by whom he had seven children; and third, Elizabeth Mendenhall.

*CHARLES S., m. Anna Mitchell, and resides at Olean, N. Y.; a highly esteemed citizen and an able lawyer; no issue.

†JOHNSON, m. Mary Hurlbert, of Livonia, Livingstone county, N. Y: and had two children ; no records:

‡MARY JANE, m. Benjamin F. Wiggins, Dentist, in Hornellsville, and has two children, Clarence and Ida.

His children were:

I. LYDIA, b. January 23, 1804. m. John Mullinger.

II. JOHN W., b. January 3, 1805. No. 226.

III. WILLIAM A., b. January 9, 1806. No. 227.

IV. NANCY W., b. June 16, 1807. m. William C. Dills.

V. DRUSILLA, b. October 26, 1808. m. Marcellus Withers.

VI. DAVID, b. January 22, 1810. No. 228.

VII. THOMAS M., b. December 16, 1812. No. 229.

VIII. JEREMIAH, b. June 7, 1814. No. 230.

IX. BENJAMIN W., b. October 1, 1816. No. 231.

X. STEPHEN C., b. April 12, 1818. Accidentally killed d. young.

XI. SALLIE A., b. November 20, 1820. m. Thomas Stevenson.

XII. SIMEON B., b. December 20, 1822. No. 232.

XIII. MARY T., b. April 4, 1824. unm.

XIV. HARVEY G., b. August 18, 1826. No. 233.

XV. JASON S.,* b. November 28, 1828.

XVI. MILTON T., b. July 22, 1831. No. 234.

*JASON S., m. Ada Smith, 1857, and had two children, both of whom d. in infancy.

No. 120.

GEORGE CARY, son of Ezra, No. 64, b. in Gurnsey county, Ohio, 1793; m. and settled in Madison county, Ohio, and d. in 1873, in Richland county, Ohio.

His children were:

I.   HENRY SHORER,* b. June 8, 1816. No. 235.

II.   SIMON BAKER,† b. October, 1817.

III.   JOHN BRADFORD,‡ b. August, 1823.

IV.   GEORGE WASHINGTON,‖ b. 1826.

V.   SARAH A., b.

No. 121.

THOMAS CARY, son of Ezra, No. 65, b. in Bridgewater, Mass., 1771; removed with parents when a child to Turner, Maine; m. Sallie Packard, and settled in Enfield, Mass., where he resided until his death; he d. 1855, aged 84 years.

---

*These four brothers weighed over 1,000 pounds, Henry S. weighing 325; they were all giants in strength.

‡SIMON BAKER, m. Lucy Ann Marks, January, 1847; lives in Marion, Grant county, Indiana.

‡JOHN BRADFORD, m. Mary Crosswait, December, 1858; had two daughters, Jennie, b. March 29, 1860; Jessie, b. January, 1862; d. April, 1863; the father d. March 4, 1863, at Lewis, Iowa.

‖GEORGE W., m. and lives at Lexington, Richland county, Ohio.

His children were :

I.   SARAH, b. 1799. m. J. P. Stearns, of Boston,
     Mass.

II. LEMUEL P.,* b. 1801.

III. EZRA, b. 1803. No. 236.

IV. CYNTHIA, b. 1805. d. unm. at Enfield, Mass.
     1862.

V.   VALORA, b. 1807. unm.

VI. EDWARD, b. 1809. No. 237.

VII. RUFUS, b. 1813. No. 238.

VIII. AURELIA, b. 1816. m. —— Brooks.

IX. MARIA F., b. 1821. unm.

No. 122.

ZACHARY CARY, son of Ezra No. 65, b. in Bridgewater,
Mass., 1773; went with parents to Turner, Maine; m. ——
Newhall, 1800; he was accidentally killed in 1809, by falling
from a building which was being raised.

*LEMUEL P., removed to Princeton, Illinois; m. and had one son who
d. 1861; the father lives at Princeton.

His children were:

I. ZACHARY, b. 1801. No. 239.

II. DAVID,* b 1803.

III. EZRA,† b. 1804.

IV. THOMAS, b. 1807. No. 240.

V. ELIZA, b. 1809. m. Lewis Barry, 1832, in Florida.

No. 123.

EZRA CARY, son of Ezra, No. 65, b. in Turner, Maine, 1780; m. Lois Staples, and resided on a farm in Turner, until his death. He d. 1853.

*DAVID, lives at Fall River, Mass. No issue.
†EZRA, d. at Phiiadelphia, Pa. No issue.

His children were :

    I.   Salmon, b. 1804. No. 241.

   II.   Seth, b. 1805. No. 242.

  III.   Daniel, b. 1806. No. 243.

  IV.   Ezra, b. 1808. d. unm.

   V.   Thomas, b. 1810. d. unm.

  VI.   Elvira, b. 1812. m. William Bradford.

 VII.   Lois, b. 1814. d. unm.

VIII.   Isabel, b. 1816. d. uum.

  IX.   Cynthia, b. 1818. d. unm.

   X.   Eunice, b. 1820. m. —— Davis, of Lisbon, Maine.

  XI.   Lydia, b. 1822. d. unm.

 XII.   Clara, b. 1824. m. Daniel Teague, of Turner, Maine.

No. 124.

John Shepherd Cary, son of Ezra, No. 65, b. in Turner, Maine, 1790 ; went to Leeds, Maine, 1809 ; was a deacon in Baptist Church ; m. a Miss Lane ; bought a farm in Leeds, on which he lived and d. His first wife d. 1826, and he m. second, the widow of General Bolster, in Paris, Maine, by whom he had one child. He was a prominent and influential citizen. Date of death unascertained.

His children were:

    I.   JOHN, b. ——— Lives in New York State.

    II. JAMES, b. ——— d. unm. at 20 years of age.

  III. ORMOND, b. ——— d. without issue 1852.

  IV. HENRY, b. 1830. m. and lives in Franklin county.
      Maine.

No. 125.

BETHUEL CARY, son of Ezra, No. 65, b. in Turner, Maine, 1793; m. Lucy Robinson, 1817, and lives in East Summer, Maine.

His children were:

    I.   LUCY ANN, b. 1818. m. Eleazer Ellis, 1836.

    II. WILLIAM, b. 1820. No. 244.

  III. BENJAMIN F., b. 1822. No. 245.

  IV. BETHUEL,* b. 1825.

    V. CYNTHIA T., b. 1830. m. Charles R. Bonney, 1855.

  VI. SARAH D., b. 1832. m. Isaac Bonney, 1854.

*BETHUEL, m. 1850. d. 1852.

No. 126.

*FRANCIS CARY, son of Major Daniel, No. 66, b. in Bridgewater, Mass., May 5, 1785; went with parents to Turner, Maine, where he m. Sarah Phillips, of Green, Maine, July 10, and resided in Turner upon a farm; greatly esteemed for his many virtues. He d. November 9, 1865, of congestion of the lungs, aged 80 years; his wife d. November 2, 1865.

His children were:

    I.   ZIBIAH,† b. June 6, 1812.

    II.   CHARLES, b. June 27, 1814. No. 246.

    III. EUNICE,‡ b. December 28, 1816.

    IV. ANN, b. September 26, 1819. d. March 5, 1843.

    V.   FRANCIS, b. September 29, 1824. No. 247.

    VI. AVEY,‖ b. August 6, 1827.

    VII. OLIVE,§ b. December 25, 1829.

   VIII. CHLOE, b. March 17, 1832. d. April 19, 1841.

*The author of these records is greatly indebted to Francis Cary for the facts in regard to the Carys of Maine. He took a great interest in the work and hoped to live to read the result. In a letter to me giving extensive tables of the family in Maine, he says: "I never knew a Cary extensively rich, and I never knew one supported by the town. I never knew one a drunkard, and they have been generally noted for their morality and piety."

†ZIBIAH, m. first, Estes W. French, December 23, 1833; and second, Elisha O. Drake.

‡EUNICE, m. Captain Hiram Bryant, May 4, 1841.

‖AVEY, m. Francis Hayes, August 12, 1856, and lives in Rhode Island.

§OLIVE, m. Thomas Scott Whitman, November 1, 1832, and has one child.

No. 127.

CASSANDER CARY, son of Dr. Luther, No. 67, b. in Turner, Maine, 1782; m. Sarah Clapp, October 12, 1808, of Turner, she d. 1817, and he m. Joanna Jones, 1818. He d. in Turner, 1831.

His children were:

I.   SOPHIA, b. April 12, 1810.   unm.

II. MARTHA, b. May 5, 1812.   m. Henry Roby, 1834.

III. HARRIET, b. August 24, 1814.   m. Thomas R. Sampson, 1841.

IV. SARAH, b. Nov'r. 14, 1816. m. Levi Booth, 1857.

V.   LUTHER, b. December 1, 1820.   No. 248.

VI. HENRY,* b. June 12, 1823.

VII. CASSANDER,† b. May 2, 1825.

VIII. CLARA, b. November 14, 1827.   m. John Martin, 1850.

No. 128.

WILLIAM CARY, son of Dr. Luther, No. 67, b. in Turner, Me., March 14, 1784; m. first, Dolly Smith, 1808, she d. in 1818; second, Lucretia Reed, 1819, she d. in 1826; third Huldah Sawyer, 1828. At last accounts he was still living in Turner, in very old age.

*HENRY, m. Ellen A. Sampson and has a family; resides in Turner, Me.
†CASSANDER, m. Mary Burrell, 1857; resides with family in Turner, Me.

His children were:

I.   NABBY, b. April 23, 1809. m. J. B. Barrell, December 30, 1828. d. August 21, 1858.

II. ALMA, b. 1810. unm. Living in Turner, Me.

III. SOPHIA L., b. 1812. unm. d. July 9, 1864.

IV. SUSAN, b. April 19, 1813. m. Waldo A. Blossom, April 19, 1835.

V.   LOUISA, b. 1816. d. in infancy.

VI. DOLLY, b. August 13, 1818. m. Rev. J. T. Howes, November, 1850.

VII. WILLIAM,* b. December 29, 1826.

VIII. JAMES A.,† b. November 15, 1830.

IX. ASA CLINTON,‡ b. May 29, 1832.

X.   ELLEN, b. 1834. unm. Teacher in Portland, Me.

XI. LUCRETIA, b. 1835. d. October 10, 1855.

XII. LUTHER KING,‖ b. 1837.

---

*WILLIAM, studied law; m. Caroline Weston; and practiced law in Galena, Illinois.

†JAMES A., m. Rosetta Kimball, 1853; has two sons, viz.: James Clinton, b. 1854, and William K., b. 1858; resides in Maine; his wife d. July 19, 1873.

‡ASA CLINTON, m. Jessie Poestlay, 1859; had a daughter, Isabella, b. 1861; resides in Fort Fairfield, Aroostock county, Me.

‖LUTHER KING, m. Ellen M. Bradford, November, 1859; had a daughter Susan, b. 1862; resides in Fort Fairfield, Aroostock county, Me.

No. 129.

ANSLEM CARY, son of Luther, No. 67, b. in Williamsburg, Mass., June 8, 1787; m. February 14, 1816, Rhoda G. Stockbridge, resided in Greene, Maine, but removed to Muskingum county, Ohio, in 1837, where he still resides. He has lived a life of probity and usefulness; is a ruling elder in the Presbyterian Church, with which denomination nearly all his family are connected. At the time of printing these memorials he is in his 87th year.

His children were:

I. HARRISON GRAY OTIS, b. December 28, 1816. No. 249.

II. SARAH AUGUSTA,* b. July 7, 1818.

III. CLARA ISABELLA STOCKBRIDGE,† b. April 24, 1820.

IV. FRANCES ANGER GAGE,‡ b. February 21, 1822.

V. LUCRETIA HELEN,‖ b. December 31, 1827.

*SARAH AUGUSTA, m. Morgan Lamson, a fruit grower, living in Chillicothe, Missouri.

†CLARA I. S., m. Alfred Barron, druggist, September 17, 1849; residing at Zanesville, Ohio; had first, Clara Augusta, b. May 1, 1851, d. November 28, 1855; second, Edward Cary, b. June 28, 1853; third, Alice Cary Stockbridge, b. August 8, 1855.

‡FRANCES A. G., m. George W. Thompson, merchant, January 22, 1845; resides at Zanesville, Ohio; had first, Alice, b. May 28, 1846; second, Mary Helen, b. September 16, 1848; third, Julietta Eva, b. November 9, 1850; fourth, Frances Anna, b. February 19, 1853, d. December 13, 1861; fifth, Augusta Clara, b. October 18, 1855; sixth, George Cary, b. January 2, 1858; seventh, Edith Cary, b. May 7, 1860; eighth, Lilian Cary, b. August 27, 1862.

‖LUCRETIA HELEN, m. James H. Lockwood, merchant, and lives in Chillicothe, Missouri.

No. 130.

ALANSON CARY, son of Dr. Luther, No. 67, b. in Turner, Maine, December 23, 1790; m. Susan Brett, July 4, 1816. He is a deacon in the church, and a very worthy citizen of Turner.

His children were:

    I. SUSAN, b. April 2, 1817. m. Harrison Blake, October 3, 1836.

    II. ALANSON,* b. March 9, 1827.

    III. CLARA E., b. May 31, 1836. m. Rev. S. G. Narcross, 1861.

No. 131.

HUGH CARY, son of Dr. Luther, No. 67, b. in Turner, Maine, October 17, 1792; m. Silena Phillips, July 7, 1816, and resides in Turner.

*ALANSON, m. a Miss Smith, September 15, 1858; resides in New York City; has one son Albert Alanson, b. July 16, 1859.

His children were:

I. LUCIE A., b. May 14, 1818. m. Jesse Follet, July 4, 1839.

II. EMILY, b. April 18, 1820. unm.

III. MAURICE, b. November 23, 1821. m. Emily T. Jones, November 27, 1862.

IV. JARIUS, b. September 25, 1823. No. 250.

V. ANNA, b. December 28, 1827. m. D. Briggs, May 31, 1853.

VI. CLARA, b. January 23, 1829. m. William L. Blake, May 31, 1853.

VII. LUTHER E., b. January 16, 1834. d. May 30, 1838.

VIII. FRANCIS A., b. January 19, 1840. unm.

No. 132.

MAURICE CARY, son of Dr. Luther, No. 67, b. in Turner, Maine, November 15, 1795; removed to Hocking county, Ohio; m. Joanna Butin, October 27, 1831; thence removed in 1839 to Iowa, near Burlington; thence to Jasper county, where he still resides.

His children were:

  I.   —— a son, b. August 4, 1835. d. same day.
 II.   MALVINA, b. April 7, 1837.
III.   LUTHER KING, b. February 27, 1839. Joined
        union army, 1861. n. t.
 IV.   JOHN COLEMAN,* b. December 6, 1841.
  V.   HARRISON, b. July 29, 1843.
 VI.   JAMES, b. December 21, 1845.
VII.   EMILY, b. May 15, 1848.
VIII. ANNA MARIA, .b. July 4, 1850.
 IX.   MAURICE, b. September 9, 1844. d. July 25,
        1855.

No. 134.

WILLIAM HOLMAN CARY, son of Ephraim, No. 68, b. in
Bridgewater, Mass., May 12, 1779; went with parents to
Maine; was a carpenter by trade; settled in Holton, Maine,
where he d. January 27, 1859. He m. Catherine, daughter
of Captain Benjamin Hascoll, 1801.

*JOHN C., belonged to 13th Iowa Regiment; was in battle of Pittsburg
Landing; d. in the army May 3, 1862.

His children were :

   I.   JONATHAN HASCOLL,* b. November 23, 1802.

   II. SHEPARD, b. July 3, 1805. No. 251.

   III. WILLIAM H., b. October 23, 1812. No. 252.

   IV. CATHERINE,† b. June 18, 1825.

No. 133.

EPHRAIM CARY, son of Ephraim, No. 68, b. in Bridge-water, Mass., 1782; went with parents to Minot, Maine; m. Anna Hill, 1809. d. ——

His children were :

   I.   LUCIUS, b. 1810. d. without issue at Minot, 1843.

   II. HORACE, b. 1811. No. 253.

   III. ANNE, b. 1815. m. Dr. N. Reed, 1853. d. 1852.

   IV. JANE, b. 1818. m. —— Wyman, 1846.

   V. CATHERINE, b. 1822. m. P. B. Chase, 1842.

†JONATHAN H., m. Eliza Haskell, December 25, 1831, at New Salem, Mass., and had one son Henry Francis.

†CATHERINE, m. Captain Isaac Bowen, U. S. A., March 25; 1845; had five children, both d. of yellow fever, at Pass Christian, New Mexico, October, 1858, and were buried at Buffalo, N. Y.

No. 135.

JOSEPH CARY, son of Lewis, No. 69, b. in Morris county, N. J., October 17, 1778; emigrated to Knox county, Ohio; m. Susan Morris, 1800; settled on a farm near Mount Vernon, O., where he d. 1843.

His children were:

I.   MAHALA, b. December 15, 1801. m. James Boyle, November 13, 1831. d. August 25, 1851.

II.   JAMES BARTLEY,* b. April 10, 1804.

III.   DANIEL MORRIS, b. June 17, 1806. No. 254.

IV.   JOANNA, b. October 12, 1808. Resides near Mt. Vernon, Ohio.

V.   AARON, b. July 19, 1811. Went to California. n.t.

VI.   MARTHA, b. May 6, 1816. m. Alvah Allen, December 7, 1837.

VII.   NANCY, b. September 9, 1819. d. October, 1820.

VIII. GEORGE LEVIS,† b. May 5, 1823.

*JAMES B., m. Jane S. Rogers, January 6, 1832; his wife d. August 22, 1856; and he m. Mary Drake, January 15, 1857; resides near Mount Vernon; has no children.

†GEORGE LEWIS, m. Margaret J. Turner, October 16, 1861; resides near Mount Vernon, O.

No. 136.

ABEL CARY, son of Lewis, No. 69, b. in Morris county, N. J., June 1781 ; m. in New Jersey ; emigrated to Indiana, where he d. about 1860. He had four sons, who emigrated to California, and all further trace is lost.

His children were :

    I.   JOHN.

    II.   WILLIAM.

    III.   BARKLEY.

    IV.   FRANKLIN.

No. 137.

LEVIS CARY, son of Lewis, No. 69, b. in Morris county, N. J., October 19, 1783 ; emigrated to Ohio, in 1816, and lived to old age near Kenton, Hardin county, O. He was an exemplary member of the Society of Friends. He m. Rachel Kirk, in 1807.

His children were:

    I.   SUSAN, b. March 4, 1808. m. —— Merriam, and is a widow.

    II.   ABEL, b. October 2, 1809. No. 255.

    III.   WILLIAM, b. August 9, 1811. Banker in Kenton, Ohio.

    IV.   AARON, b. August 1813. No. 256.

    V.   EDMOND, b. October 27, 1815. No. 257.

    VI.   ISABELLA, b. September 14, 1817.

    VII.   SARAH, b. October 4, 1819. d. September 30, 1841.

    VIII.   GEORGE, b. August 4, 1821. No. 258.

    IX.   BENJAMIN L., November 21, 1824. d. October 10, 1847.

No. 138.

AARON CARY, son of Lewis, No. 69, b. in Morris county, N. J., September 26, 1785; m. Phebe Thompson, 1811; removed to Bucyrus, Crawford county, O., 1828; thence to Indiana, where he d. 1842.

His children were :

- I. SARAH W., b. August 9, 1812. d. uum. September 12, 1831.
- II. LUCILLA, b. January 14, 1814. m. Ansel Dickinson, 1825, lives in Wisconsin.
- III. HANNAH, b. November 13, 1816. d. 1819.
- IV. STEPHEN J.,* b. January 14, 1819.
- V. LEVIS, b. July 20, 1821. Lives in Calusa, California. unm.
- VI. HANNAH, b. October 13, 1823. m. —— Clark, Living in California.
- VII. JANE W., b. June 15, 1827. m. Dr. J. Howard, San Francisco, California.
- VIII. JACOB T., b. January 13, 1830. d. in youth.
- IX. SARAH W., b. January 27, 1832. m. H. W. Williams, Calusa, California.

No. 139.

JOHN CARY, son of Lewis No. 69, born in Morris county, N. J., March 7, 1788 ; moved to Ohio ; settled on a farm in Morrow county, where he d. December 2, 1860. He m. Margaret A. Snook, January 30, 1811 ; she d. February 5, 1858.

*STEPHEN J., m. and removed to Council Bluffs, Iowa, where he d. 1855, leaving one daughter, Ida.

His children were:

   I.   LYDIA, b. March 13, 1812. d. May 13, 1812.

  II. LEVIS HENRY, b. March 27, 1813. No. 259.

 III. ISABEL CARSON, b. December 6, 1815. d. April 9, 1844.

 IV. WILLIAM S., b. May 16, 1818. No. 260.

  V. JOHN R., b. August 7, 1820. No. 261.

 VI. GEORGE C., b. March 20, 1823. No. 262.

VII. ANN E.,* b. March 19, 1825.

VIII. MARGARET J.,† b. May 13, 1828.

 IX. LURANY E., b. September 10, 1830. unm. Chesterville, O.

  X. CHARLES P., b. November 23, 1836. d. June 5, 1861.

No. 140.

DANIEL CARY, son of Lewis, No. 69, b. in Morris county, N. J., May 29, 1793; m. Eliza Wills, 1821; lives on the old homestead, near Drakesville, N. J.

*ANN E., m. Alfred Beamer, March 1, 1859; resides with family at Chesterville, Morrow county, O.

†MARGARET J., m. Isaac Coleman, October 12, 1848; resides at Brandon, Knox county, O.

His children were:

    I.   WILLIAM SAYRE, b. 1822. No. 263.

    II. SAMUEL WILLS,* b. 1824.

    III. CORNELIA, b. 1826. unm.

No. 141.

GEORGE L. CARY, son of Lewis, No. 69, b. in Morris county, N. J.,· May 29, 1799; emigrated to Wyandotte county, Ohio; m. Lucinda Halsey, 1826; and lives at Marseilles in that county.

His children were:

    I.   HENRY H., b. March 4, 1827. m. 1857, Wyandotte county, Ohio.

    II. MARY, b. May 16, 1837. Living with parents.

    III. ELIZABETH, b. May 6, 1841. m. John Cope, 1859.

    IV. EUGENIA L., b. November 17, 1843. Living with parents.

*SAMUEL W., graduated at Princeton, N. J.; studied law, and is a member of the bar in the City of New York. unm.

No. 142.

ZENAS CARY, son of Aaron, No. 70, b. at Colerain, Mass., November 26, 1782 ; was a soldier in the war of 1812, and in 1867, was still living a highly respected, honorable, christian man in the town of his nativity. He m. Sally Maxom, in 1807.

His children were:

I.   CHARLOTTE, b. September 27, 1808.   m. George Dunton.

II.   JOHN, b. July 24, 1810.   No. 264.

III.   GEORGE, b. July 4, 1812.   No. 265.

IV.   WILLIAM W., b. February 24, 1815.   No. 266.

V.   DAVID,* b. July 26, 1817.

VI.   MARIETTA, b. March 27, 1820.   d. January 6, 1832.

VII.   LEVI, b. April 2, 1822.   No. 267.

VIII.   JOSEPH E., b. May 24, 1825.   d. February 5, 1833.

No. 143.

ZÉBULON CARY, son of Josiah, No. 72, b. at Brookfield, Mass., October 5, 1781 ; m. Polly ———— in 1808. He d. in Brookfield, September 13, 1847 ; his vidow d. June 10, 1854.

---

*DAVID, m. Laura Lamb; had five children; moved to Valparaiso, Indiana. No other record.

His children were:

I.   MARY ANN, b. February 5, 1809. m. Solomon Sibley, of Prescott, Mass.

II.   JOSIAH, b. July, 1811. d. December 13, 1812.

III.   EUNICE, b. November 3, 1812. m. S. O. Johnson, of West Brookfield, Mass.

IV.   JOSIAH, b. September 29, 1814. No. 268.

V.   ZEBULON, b. September 11, 1817. d. September 10, 1822.

VI.   SUSANNA, b. July 5, 1819. m. Thomas Wheeler, of Prescott, Mass.

VII.   CALVIN E., b. May 6, 1821. d. July 11, 1823.

VIII.   ZEBULON E.,* b. April 27, 1823.

IX.   HARRIET, b. December 8, 1824. unm. West Brookfield, Mass.

X.   LUCY, b. December 10, 1826. m. Nelson B. Gale, of Wardsboro, Vt.

XI.   SARAH A., b. September 11, 1828. m. E. Kent, of Vermont.

XII.   ELIZA S., b. January 11, 1831. m. Alfred Gorham, of Barre, Mass.

XIII.   EPHRAIM C.,† b. March 10, 1833.

XIV.   LYDIA H.,‡ b. September 10, 1835.

*ZEBULON E., m. Elizabeth Garland; lives in West Brookfield, Mass. No issue.

†EPHRAIM C. unm. Was in 34th Regiment of Massachusetts Volunteers.

‡LYDIA H., m. John Davis, September 28, 1864; had two children; Herbert C., b. July 15, 1860; and John A., b. March 7, 1870. Mother d. March 27, 1870.

No. 144.

JOSIAH CARY, son of Josiah, No. 72, b. in West Brookfield, Mass., April 7, 1783; m. Betsy Henry, May 3, 1807;
he d. in St. Charles, Mo., March 8, 1861.

His children were:

   I.   HENRY WATSON, b. 1811.   d. September 24,
         1827.

   II. JOSIAH ADDISON, b. 1813. No. 269.

   III. CAROLINE E., b. 1815. m. Rev. A. V. C. Schenck.

   IV. CHARLES AUGUSTUS, b. 1817. d. March 9, 1847.

No. 145.

AVERY CARY, son of Josiah, No. 72, b. at Brookfield,
Mass., February 17, 1789; m. Abiah Spooner, of West
Brookfield.

His children were:

   I.   MARTHA B., b. 1811. m. Ebenezer Dunham,
         Pittsfield, Mass.

   II. NATHAN C., b. 1814. No. 270.

   III. MARY, b. 1816. m. —— Noble.

   IV. ELIZABETH C., b. 1820. m. S. R. Darling,
         Elyria, O.

   V. SAMUEL A., b. 1823. No. 271.

   VI. JOSIAH W., b. 1828. n. t.

No. 146.

JONATHAN CARY, son of Josiah, No. 72, b. in Brookfield, Mass., September 10, 1798; m. first, Lucy H. Ayres, April 27, 1825; second, Betsy P. Ward, October 16, 1834; and resides in Worcester, Mass.

His children were:

    I.   WILLIAM AYRES,* b. June 3, 1826.

    II. FREELOVE, b. April 11, 1829. m. David C. Thurston, 1854.

No. 147.

THOMAS H. CARY, son of Josiah, No. 72, b. in Brookfield, Mass., August 15, 1802; m. Hannah Moulton, of Brookfield, March 25, 1828; removed to Springville, N. Y., where he still resides.

His children were:

    I.   DANIEL M., b. June 25, 1831. No. 272.

    II. JULIA A., b. December 20, 1833. d. May 16, 1853.

    III. CHARLES,† b. February 25, 1838.

---

*WILLIAM A., m. Harriet Parker, November, 1851, and had one daughter, Gertrude, b. October 28, 1859.

†CHARLES, m. Matilda Hanley, December 1, 1862; and resides at Springville, N. Y.

No. 148.

Leonard Cary, son of Recompence, No. 73, b. in Ward, Mass., April 2. 1793; was a mechanic; was twice m. and had three children by each wife. He d. in Boston, Mass., April 27, 1846.

His children were:

 I. Preston Moore,* b. August 15, 1816.

 II. Martha E.,† b. September 1, 1819.

 III. Caroline R.,‡ b. December 17, 1822.

 IV. Mary A.,‖ b. 1824.

 V. Harriet E., b. November 15, 1827. d.

 VI. Charles Hibben, b. October 5, 1829. n. t.

No. 149.

Barzillai Cary, son of Moses, No. 74, b. in Bridge-water, Mass., August 25, 1780; m. Vashti, daughter of Nathan Snell, 1808; lived a respectable farmer in Bridgewater, and d. there 1852.

---

*Preston M., was in Savannah, Georgia, at the beginning of the civil war, and know nothing of him since; his only son, Charles Preston, was in the Union Army.

†Martha, m. —— Ellis; had one daughter, now living in Holden, Mass. Martha d. several years since.

‡Caroline R., m. William Haskell; and lives in North Brookfield.

‖Mary Ann, m. —— Johnson, and is living a widow in North Brookfield, Mass.

His children were:

I.   SUSANNA, b. 1808.   m. Luke Perkins, of Auburn, Mass.

II.   BETSY, b. 1810.   m. James Copeland, of West Bridgewater.

III.   ALMIRA, b. 1812.   m. Edward S. Packard.   d. 1843.

IV.   BARZILLAI,* b. 1815.

V.   NATHAN S.,† b. 1817.

VI.   LUCIUS,‡ b. 1819.

VII.   RHODA, b. 1821.   m. Daniel S. Howard.

VIII.   VESTOR S., b. 1822.   m. H. K. Keith, of Kingston, Mass.

IX.   MARY, b. 1823.   m. S. W. Clapp, Boston, Mass.

No. 150.

CALEB CARY, son of Jonathan, No. 75, b. in Bridgewater, Mass., 1788; removed to East Machias, Maine, in 1809; m. Sarah J. Talbor; he d. December 20, 1848; his widow d. 1856.

*BARZILLAI, m. Augusta Gurney; resides on the homestead; has two daughters, Helen Augusta and Louisa Francis.

†NATHAN S., m. Betsy Gurney; resides in Bridgewater; has one daughter, Mary Alice.

‡LUCIUS, m. first, Elizabeth Gilham; and second, Martha Stone; removed to Missouri; had three sons, but have no trace of them.

His children were :

 I. CHARLES, b. 1826. No. 273.

 II. LUCY d. in infancy.

 III. LEVIS S.,* b. 1835.

No. 151.

JONATHAN CARY, son of Jonathan, No. 75, b. in Bridge-
water, Mass., 1791 ; removed when young to East Machias,
Maine ; m. Mary Handscomb, 1818, and settled in Cooper,
Maine. Living at last advice.

His children were :

 I. ELISHA CALEB, b. about 1819. No. 274.

 II. HENRY SMITH, b. about 1821. No. 275.

 III. MARY H.,† b. about 1823.

 IV. PRISCILLA P.,‡ b. about 1825.

 V. AARON H., b. about 1827. d. young.

*LEWIS S., m. Lavina Simpson, 1860 ; resides in East Machias; has
one son, Wales L., b. 1861.

†MARY H. m. Samuel Sprague, in 1844; and had eight children.

‡PRISCILLA P., m. Nelson Bridgham, 1846 ; and had seven children.

No. 152.

LUTHER CARY, son of Jonathan, No. 75, b. in Bridge-water, Mass., 1794; removed when young to East Machias, Maine; m. Eliza W. Foster, 1818; settled in Cooper, Maine, and still lives.

His children were:

I. JAMES WEBBER, b. August, 1819. No. 276.

II. ELIZA A., b. April, 1822. d. May, 1827.

·III. GEORGE WILLIAMS,* b. August, 1824.

IV. MARY L., b. November, 1826. d. July, 1827.

V. DELIA F.,† b. June, 1828.

VI. CHARLOTTE A,‡ b. December, 1830.

VII. MARY E.,‖ b. March, 1834.

VIII. MARTIN L., b. September, 1836. In Union army.

IX. MARTHA E, b. April, 1838. at Providence, R. I.

X. HIRAM FOSTER, b. August, 1842. In Union army.

*GEORGE W., m. Roxana Damon, 1855; and resides in Cooper, Maine.
†DELIA F., m. Stephen J. Getchel, of Cooper, Maine, October, 1853; and has three children.
‡CHARLOTTE A., m. Henry L. Foster, 1858; and resides in Providence, Rhode Island.
‖MARY E., m. Charles Cary, of East Machias, Maine; and had two children.

No. 153.

MARTIN CARY, son of Jonathan, No. 75, b. in Bridge-water, Mass., 1795; m. Bethia, daughter of Deacon Ichabod Howard, 1822; and settled in North Bridgewater, Mass.

His children were:

I.   MELINDA, b. 1825. m. Benjamin C. Fribisher.

II.   HENRY MARTIN, b. 1827. d. 1829.

III.   GEORGE CLARK,* b. 1831.

IV.   CHARLES HOWARD,† b. 1837.

No. 154.

ALPHEUS CARY, son of Alpheus, No. 76, born at Quincy, Mass., November 5, 1788; m. Deborah Thayer; devoted his life to teaching; spent many years in Quincy, but when last heard from was living a widower, and childless in Boston, Mass.

His children were:

I.   ALPHEUS, b. October, 1827. d. September, 1836.

II.   GEORGE WASHINGTON, b. 1830. d. October, 1850.

III.   CHARLES WILLIAM, b. 1833. d. February, 1840.

Name extinct in this branch.

*GEORGE C., m. Harriet G. Ford, 1855; lives in North Bridgewater; had one son, Henry Martin, b. 1857.

†CHARLES H., m. Hannah C. Alden, 1858; lives in North Bridgewater; had one son, Martin Alden, b. 1860.

No. 155.

LEWIS CARY, son of Alpheus, No. 76, b. in Quincy, Mass., March 31, 1798 ; m. Adeline E. Billings, 1821, in Boston, Mass. He d. November, 1834.

His children were:
- I. LEWIS B.,* b. 1822.
- II. CHARLES G., b. 1824. No. 277.
- III. THOMAS W., b. 1826. No. 278.

No. 156.

ISAAC CARY, son of Alpheus, No. 76, b. in Quincy, Mass., June 25, 1802 ; m. Julia, daughter of Simon Willard, (the celebrated clock maker), 1830 ; removed to Boston, Mass., and was for more than thirty years an engraver of bank notes, and manager and treasurer of the American Bank Note Co. He was a member of the Board of Aldermen for seventeen consecutive years, and held various city, county and state offices. His first wife d. in 1863 ; he m. Mariam White, (Priest), daughter of Hon. Josiah Stedman, of Boston.

LEWIS BILLINGS, m. Caroline Boston ; and had one daughter, Adeline Eliza, who d. in infancy.

His children were :

I.   ABIGAIL PERKINS, b. January, 1832. d. January, 1857.

- II.   ALEXANDER CLAXTON, b. February, 1834. No. 279.

III.   JULIA KNOX, b. August, 1836.

IV.   MARY WILLARD, b. July, 1838.

V.   ISAAC, b. April, 1840.

VI.   HARRIET; b. April, 1842.

No. 157.

OTIS CARY, son of James, No. 77, b. in Bridgewater, Mass., June 14, 1804; m. Mary Dodge, daughter of Captain Joseph Terry, 1830. He resides in Foxboro, Mass., has been for many years an extensive manufacturer ; and has been frequently a member of both branches of the Legislature ; a prominent, popular and useful citizen.

His children were;

I.   MARY ANN, b. 1831.   m. Arza B. Keith, of Bridgewater, Mass.

II. SARAH T., b. 1834.

III. JOHN, b. 1836. uum. d. at Philadelphia, 1862.

IV. HANNAH, b. 1840.

V.   CHARLES,* b. 1842.

VI. GEORGE, b. 1844. d. 1849.

VII. OTIS, b. 1851.

No. 158.

AUSTIN CARY, son of James, No. 77, b. in Bridgewater, Mass., 1809; graduated at Amherst College, in 1837; studied theology; settled as a Congregational Minister, in Sunderland; m. Catherine, daughter of Roger Phelps, of Windsor, Ct., 1842; d. much lamented, 1849; his widow m. Rev. M. Kingman, of Claremont, N. H.

His children were:

I.   AUSTIN P., b. 1846.

II. WILLIE C., b. 1848.

*CHARLES, graduated at Amherst College; went to Philadelphia, and is of the well-known house of Wood & Cary.

No. 159.

ABRAM CARY, son of Isaac, No. 78, b. in Morris county, N. J., 1762 ; m. in New Jersey ; removed to Pennsylvania, thence to the Northwest Territory, settling in Cincinnati, in 1796; was sheriff and jailer in Cincinnati ; owned a tract of land in Millcreek Valley, now part of the city; he removed early in the present century to Springfield, Clark county, O., where he d. 1816.

His children were:

I.   COLONEL SAMUEL, b. 1784. No. 280.
II.   WAITSELL MUNSON, b. 1785. No. 281.
III.   SARAH, b. 1788.
IV.   PHEBE,* b. 1790.
V.   CHARLOTTE, b. 1892. n. t.
VI.   MARTHA, b. 1794. m. d. childless, Springfield, Ohio.
VII.   FRANCIS, b. 1786. A Methodist Clergyman. n. t.
VIII.   MARTHA, b. 1798. n. t.
IX.   ELIZA, b. 1800. n. t.

No. 160.

HENRY CARY, son of John, No. 79, b. in Mendham, N. J , January 6, 1780 ; m. Sarah Day, February 9, 1802 ; removed to West Pennsylvania in 1806; was a farmer; d. 1853 ; his wife d. 1859.

---

*PHEBE, m. ——— Skillman, and had five sons and three daughters.

His children were;

I. REBECCA, b. January 7, 1804. m. J. Connet, Green county, Pa.

II. DAVID, b. April 16, 1808. d. October 29, 1814.

III. BETHANY, b. February 4, 1812. m. —— Jordan, Athens county, Ohio.

IV. JOHN,* b. January 11, 1815.

V. ISAAC N.,† b. March 22, 1816.

No. 161.

CLEMENT CARY, son of John, No. 79, b. in Mendham, N. J., May 22, 1792; lived on a farm in Suckasunny' Plains, N. J. He m. first, Phebe Jennings, and had by her seven children; second, Thankful Hathaway, and had by her one child; third, Julia King; he survived his third wife, and died 1854.

---

*JOHN, is a physician in Green county, Pa.; has one daughter.

†ISAAC N., is a Cumberland Presbyterian Minister, at Carmichael's, Green county, Pa.

His children were:

    I.   MARY ANN, b. September 29, 1806. m. Albert
           Mathews, in Orange county, N. J.

   II.   SILAS JENNINGS,* b. January 1, 1808.

  III.   EBENEZER,† b. July 30, 1810.

  IV.   REBECCA P.,‡ b. February 13, 1813.

   V.   ELIZABETH D., b. July 9, 1815. Teacher in Cali-
           fornia. unm.

  VI.   DANIEL LYON, b. July 21, 1817. Went to Cali-
           fornia.

 VII.   PHEBE J., b. December 25, 1819. m. D. G.
           Smith, Orange county, N. J.

VIII.   RALPH HATHAWAY, b. March 8, 1827. n. t.

No. 162

NATHANIEL CARY, son of John, No. 79, b. in Mendham,
N. J., December 5, 1786 ; m. Matilda Axtell, 1814; removed
to Newark, N. J., 1856, and was living there at last account.

*SILAS J., m. Miss Dougherty, and had by her two children : his wife
and children both d.; he moved to Clinton, Miss., settled there as a merchant ; m. a second wife, and had by her two children, of whom I have no
trace ; he d. of cholera en route to New York city.

†EBENEZER, went to Augusta, Ga.; was a carriage maker ; m. and had
children there. n. t.

‡REBECCA, m. Lewis Lyon, of Newark, N. J. d. August 7, 1853.

His children were:

I.   HENRY AXTEL, b. November 4, 1816.   No. 282.

II.   MARYETTE,* b. February 3, 1819.

III.   LEVIS, b. June 13, 1820.   No. 283.

IV.   ISAAC, b. March 22, 1823.   No. 284.

V.   JOHN,† b. November 29, 1825.

VI.   MATILDA, b. February 11, 1828.   d. January 31, 1830.

VII.   MATILDA, b. January 3, 1830. unm.

VIII.   NATHANIEL, b. April 22, 1832. d. March 15, 1833.

IX.   ELIAS RIGGS,‡ b. May 25, 1833.

X.   DAVID LYON, b. January 25, 1837.   d. February 10, 1846.

No. 163.

JOHN CARY, son of John No. 79, b. in Mendham, N. J., May 27, 1797; m. Eunice H. Babbitt, 1819; occupied part of the old homestead farm, owned by his grandfather, John, No. 38. In furnishing a history of his grandfather's family he

---

*MARYETTE, m. W. F. Morrow, 1838; has a large family; and resides near St. Joseph, Michigan.

†JOHN, m. Martha E. Axtel, February 12, 1862; lives in Newark, N. J. No records.

‡ELIAS R., m. Amanda Perine, November 23, 1859; was a surgeon in the army. No records.

says: " I have never known a Cary very wealthy, nor very poor, and never heard of one charged with crime."

His children were :

   I. JOANNA,* b. August 17, 1821.

   II. ELIZABETH,† b. November 9, 1822.

   III. EZRA DAY, b. February 11, 1824. d. August 31, 1827.

   IV. DAVID HOVELL, b. October 5, 1825. d. September 6, 1827.

   V. LOUISA, b. April 24, 1827. d. March, 1854.

   VI. SARAH J.,‡ b. September 17, 1828.

   VII. EZRA H.,‖ b. June 25, 1830.

   VIII. MARTHA, b. July 4, 1832. d. September 5, 1833.

   IX. JOHN H., b. April 2, 1835. d. September 13, 1837.

   X. EDWIN H., b. April 24, 1837.

   XI. MARY F., b. October 7, 1839. With parents. unm.

---

*JOANNA, m. 1845, Dr. Henry Vigor; had ten children; lives in Fayette county, Ohio.

†ELIZABETH, m. Stephen Lyon, September 29, 1850; has two children, and lives at Martinsville, Somerset county, N. J.

‡SARAH J., graduated at Mount Holyoke Seminary, Mass.; taught at Port Jarvis, N. Y.

‖EZRA H., graduated at Medical College, at Cincinnati, and was surgeon in the Potomac Army.

No. 164.

ISAAC CARY, son of John, No. 79, b. in Mendham, N. J., November 18, 1800 ; m. Sarah B. Hovey, Richmond, Va., September 11, 1831 ; extensively engaged in carriage manufacturing.

His children were:

I.   FRANCIS ANN, b. July 17, 1832.   d. June 23, 1856.

II.   ELLOR VIRGINIA, b. October 17, 1838.   d. August 16, 1842.

III.   MARY JULIA, b. October 19, 1841.   d. July, 1842.

The name of Cary extinct in this branch.

No. 165.

EBENEZER CARY, son of Ebenezer, No. 80, b. in Western New York, about 1816; m. Catherine J. Fonda ; he d. November, 1863.

His children were:

I.   ALFRED.   n. t.

II.   EBENEZER.   n. t.

III.   LUCINDA.   n. t.

IV.   JOHN.   n. t.

says: " I have never known a Cary very wealthy, nor very poor, and never heard of one charged with crime."

His children were:

I. JOANNA,* b. August 17, 1821.

II. ELIZABETH,† b. November 9, 1822.

III. EZRA DAY, b. February 11, 1824. d. August 31, 1827.

IV. DAVID HOWELL, b. October 5, 1825. d. September 6, 1827.

V. LOUISA, b. April 24, 1827. d. March, 1854.

VI. SARAH J.,‡ b. September 17, 1828.

VII. EZRA H.,| b. June 25, 1830.

VIII. MARTHA, b. July 4, 1832. d. September 5, 1833.

IX. JOHN H., b. April 2, 1835. d. September 13, 1837.

X. EDWIN H., b. April 24, 1837.

XI. MARY F., b. October 7, 1839. With parents, unm.

*JOANNA, m. 1845, Dr. Henry Vigor: had ten children: lives in Fayette county, Ohio.

†ELIZABETH, m. Stephen Lyon, September 29, 1850; has two chil-

No. 164.

Isaac Cary, son of John, No. 79, b. in Mendham, N. J., November 18, 1800; m. Sarah B. Hovey, Richmond, Va., September 11, 1831; extensively engaged in carriage manufacturing.

His children were:

I.   Francis Ann, b. July 17, 1832.   d. June 23, 1856.
II. Ellor Virginia, b. October 17, 1838.   d. August 16, 1842.
III. Mary Julia, b. October 19, 1841.   d. July, 1842.

The name of Cary extinct in this branch.

No. 165.

Ebenezer Cary, son of Ebenezer, No. 80, b. in Western New York, about 1816; m. Catherine J. Fonda; he d. November, 1863.

His children were:

I.   Alfred.   n. t.
II. Ebenezer.   n. t.
III. Lucinda.   n. t.
IV. John.   n. t.

says: "I have never known a Cary very wealthy, nor very poor, and never heard of one charged with crime."

His children were:

    I.   JOANNA,* b. August 17, 1821.

    II.   ELIZABETH,† b. November 9, 1822.

    III.   EZRA DAY, b. February 11, 1824. d. August 31, 1827.

    IV.   DAVID HOVELL, b. October 5, 1825. d. September 6, 1827.

    V.   LOUISA, b. April 24, 1827. d. March, 1854.

    VI.   SARAH J.,‡ b. September 17, 1828.

    VII.   EZRA H.,‖ b. June 25, 1830.

    VIII.   MARTHA, b. July 4, 1832. d. September 5, 1833.

    IX.   JOHN H., b. April 2, 1835. d. September 13, 1837.

    X.   EDWIN H., b. April 24, 1837.

    XI.   MARY F., b. October 7, 1839. With parents. unm.

---

*JOANNA, m. 1845, Dr. Henry Vigor; had ten children; lives in Fayette county, Ohio.

†ELIZABETH, m. Stephen Lyon, September 29, 1850; has two children, and lives at Martinsville, Somerset county, N. J.

‡SARAH J., graduated at Mount Holyoke Seminary, Mass.; taught at Port Jarvis, N. Y.

‖EZRA H., graduated at Medical College, at Cincinnati, and was surgeon in the Potomac Army.

No. 164.

Isaac Cary, son of John, No. 79, b. in Mendham, N. J., November 18, 1800 ; m. Sarah B. Hovey, Richmond, Va., September 11, 1831 ; extensively engaged in carriage manufacturing.

His children were:

I. Francis Ann, b. July 17, 1832. d. June 23, 1856.

II. Ellor Virginia, b. October 17, 1838. d. August 16, 1842.

III. Mary Julia, b. October 19, 1841. d. July, 1842.

The name of Cary extinct in this branch.

No. 165.

Ebenezer Cary, son of Ebenezer, No. 80, b. in Western New York, about 1816; m. Catherine J. Fonda ; he d. November, 1863.

His children were :

I. Alfred. n. t.

II. Ebenezer. n. t.

III. Lucinda. n. t.

IV. John. n. t.

No. 166.

Ebenezer Cary, son of Chad, No. 81, b. at Smithfield, R. I., August 6, 1797; was a machinist; m. first, Rhoda Burlingame, of Situate, R. I., January 3, 1821; second, Adah Burlingame, a sister of first wife.

His children were:

 I.   Hannah B.,* b. October 14, 1821.

 II.   Elizabeth,† b. August 4, 1823.

 III. George, b. August 4, 1825. d. in infancy.

 IV.   Angeline,‡ b. September 29, 1827.

 V.   Abby T., b. February 8, 1830. d. in infancy.

 VI.   Emily T., b. February 8, 1831. unm. in Providence, R. I.

 VII. Susan,‖ b. May 30, 1833.

 VIII. Ester A.,§ b. May 8, 1836.

 IX.   Jerome, b. 1838. d. in infancy.

 X.   Ellen M.,(a) b. May 13, 1841.

 XI.   Isabel, b. November 19, 1851. unm. in Providence, R. I.

*Hannah, m. John M. Barker, November 24, 1856, Providence, R. I., who distinguished himself as a soldier and officer in the Union Army.

Elizabeth, m. Joel G. Brown, December 31, 1846; now a widow in Providence, R. I.

‡Angeline, m. Edward D. Leveck, May 2, 1847; resides in Providence, R. I.

‖Susan, m. Henry Young, November 27, 1851; has three children; resides in Providence, R. I.

§Ester A., m. Thomas J. Thurber, September, 1854; has two children; resides in Woonsocket, R. I.

(a) Ellen M., m. Dan'l Perkins, July 25. 1864; resides in Providence, R. I.

No. 167.

WILLIAM CARY, son of Chad, No. 80, b. in Smithfield, R. I., March 18, 1799; was a stone cutter by trade; m. Elmer, daughter of Olney Colwell, of Johnston, R. I., August 14, 1836; d. August 21, 1862, at Pine Hill, Johnstown, R. I.

His children were:

I. WILLIAM HENRY, b. May 17, 1837. No. 285.

II. OLNEY C., b. July 15, 1840. d. February 30, 1842.

III. JOHN O., b. August 27, 1841. d. August 25, 1843.

IV. JULIA,* b. November 27, 1843.

V. SARAH E., b. July 30, 1845. d. May 2, 1846.

VI. MARY M., } b. December { d. January 22, 1851.
VII. URSULA L., } 10, 1850. { d. February 19, 1851.

VIII. NATHANIEL S., b. January 25, 1852. Living at South Providence, R. I.

IX. GEORGE W., b. May 8, 1854. Lived at Graniteville, Johnston, R. I.

X. RODOLPHO, b. February 17, 1858. Living at S. Providence, R. I.

*JULIA, m. Rufus Harris, May 11, 1862; has three children living at Graniteville, R. I.

No· 168.

GEORGE S. CARY, son of Chad. No. 81, b. at Smithfield, R. I., September 6, 1801 ; m. Sarah, daughter of Capt. Joseph Alverson, of Johnstown, R. I., February 6, 1825 ; removed to Cleveland, O., where he still resides.

His children were :

    I.   MALISSA A.,* b. December 7, 1826.

    II.   GEORGE W., b. June 11, 1829. No 286.

    III.   WILLIAM H., b. August 31, 1831. No. 287.

    IV.   EDVARD M., b. April 28, 1834. No. 288.

No. 169.

CHAD. B. CARY, son of Chad. No. 81, b. in Johnstown, R. I., April 7, 1813; m. Ann Field, of Pomfret, Ct., July 14, 1831 ; was by occupation a fancy painter; he d. in Oxford, Mass., March 29, 1855.

*MALISSA A., m. James W. Spifield, M. D., May 10, 1846; had four children ; present address, No. 180 Franklin Street, New York city.

His children were:

I.   GEORGE A., b. June 23, 1832. d. in Oxford,
     Mass., January 3, 1858.

II. ALBERT, b. September 27, 1837. d. in Killingly,
     Ct., July 28, 1838.

III. CHARLES F.,* b. April 1, 1839.

IV. FREDERICK E., b. April 6, 1841. d. at Worcester,
     Mass., October 5, 1860.

V.   HELEN E.,† b. February, 1843.

VI. EMMA J.,‡ b. May 3, 1845.

VII. FRANCES A., b. February 14, 1847. d. at Wor-
     cester, Mass., April 15, 1866.

VIII. EDVARD D., b. September 9, 1849. d. at Wor-
     cester, Mass., May 1, 1865.

IX. MARA A., b. January 7, 1852. At Worcester.

No. 170.

JOHN H. CARY, son of Chad. No. 81, b. in Johnstown,
R. I., May 17, 1816; m. Sarah Lizey, of Stockport, Eng.,
November 39, 1843; was by occupation a wheelwright; lives
at No. 97 Dean street, Providence, R. I.

*CHARLES F., m. Emeline J. Burnett, June 10, 1862; had one child,
Gertrude L., b. July 10, 1863; d. February 10, 1864. He d. at Worcester,
Mass., December 14, 1865.

†HELEN E., m. Joseph A. Moore, October 10, 1867; lives at Worcester,
Mass.,

‡EMMA J., m. George E. Murdock, November 29, 1864; she d. without
issue, in Worcester, Mass., April 29, 1868.

His children were :

   I.   Edvard T., b. October 31, 1844. d. January 13, 1847

   II.   Edvin T., b. January 25, 1848. Druggist in Providence, R. I.

   III.   Alfred H., b, January 22, 1850. Printer in Providence, R. I.

   IV.   John H., b. February 10, 1853. Clerk in Providence, R. I.

   V.   Sarah A., b. February 1, 1856. d. February 16, 1856.

   VI.   Sarah Etta, b. September 30, 1862. Lives at No. 97 Dean street, Providence, R. I.

No. 171.

Joseph Cary, son of Joseph, No. 82, b, in Middlesfield, Mass., January 17, 1784 ; m. Freelove Fuller, January 20, 1803 ; removed to Ontario county, N. Y., where he resided in 1865.

His children were :

   I.   Joseph, b. September 6, 1805. Lives at Stow, Vt.

   II.   Lyman, b 1807. Lives at Stow, Vt.

   III.   Elliott, b. 1809. Lives at Stow, Vt.

No. 172.

ISAAC CARY, son of Joseph, No. 82, b. in Middlesfield, Mass., September 15, 1804; m. Sarah Wyart, in 1825; removed to Ontario county, N. Y., thence to Stow, Vt., where he resided in 1865.

His children were;

I. SARAH,* b. September 6, 1826.

II. ISAAC,† b. August 29, 1829.

III. ELIZABETH,‡ b. March 28, 1833.

IV. MARY,‖ b. July 12, 1835.

V. HUDSON, b. April 1, 1838.

VI. JOSEPH, b. Nov. 4, 1843.

VII. JANE, b. March 19, 1845.

No. 173.

RICHARD M. CARY, son of Richard, No. 83, b. in Williamsburg, Mass., December 19, 1794; m. Susanna Rice, March 12, 1815; removed to Erie county, N. Y., thence to Rock county, Wisconsin, where he d. October 17, 1868.

*SARAH, m. James Barns; had six children; resides in Ontaria, N. Y.

†ISAAC, m. —— Richardson; has one daughter; resides at Fort Edward, N. Y.

‡ELIZABETH, m. A. Harris; has two sons and two daughters; resides at Fort Edward, N. Y.

‖MARY, m. —— Prescott; has two children; lives at Stow, Vt.

His children were:

    I.   CALVIN, b. October 1, 1816.   No. 289.

    II.   EPHRAIM, b. October 27, 1818.   No. 290.

    III.   BENJAMIN T., b. February 15, 1821.   No. 291.

    IV.   ABRAHAM J.,* b. August 7, 1822.

    V.   RICHARD M., b. August 23, 1824.   d. January 3, 1825.

    VI.   LYDIA J., b. November 11, 1825. d. July 24, 1828.

    VII.   ORINDA P., b. January 29, 1828. d. February 11, 1844.

    VIII.   RICHARD, b. April 8, 1830.   No. 292.

    IX.   LYDIA S., b. February 12, 1832.   m. F. E. Osborne, January 1, 1853.

    X.   MELVIN, b. June 28, 1834.   No. 293.

    XI.   LOUISA J., b. April 22, 1837.   m. G. G. Clark, Janesville, Wisconsin.

    XII.   ROSVELL, b. January 13, 1839. d. February 14, 1868.

No. 174.

LUTHER H. CARY, son of Richard, No. 83, b. in Williamsburg, Mass., February, 1800; m. Lucy Doolittle, December, 1821; resides in Boston, Erie county, N. Y.

*ABRAHAM J., m. Elizabeth Fuller, March 26, 1857; resides in Johnstown, Wisconsin; has a son, Benjamin Franklin, b. September 3, 1858.

His children were:

    I.   Luther H.,* b. June 28, 1823.

    II. VanRensalaer,† b. August 23, 1825.

    III. Richard L.,‡ b. February 11, 1827.

    IV. Talcott P.,‖ b. April 11, 1828.

    V.   Amzi B.,§ b. August 3, 1830.

    VI. Eugene B.,(*a*) b. February 20, 1835.

No. 175.

Truman Cary, son of Asa, No. 85, b. in Williamsburg, Mass., May 31, 1791; m. Fanny Alger, of Cazenovia, N. Y., November 4, 1813; his wife d. April 28, 1864; he was living when last heard from, in Boston, Erie county, N. Y.

*Luther H., m. Arvilla Ferguson, September, 1846; went to Fon Du Lac, Wisconsin; was a surgeon in the army; now resides in San Francisco, Cal.; his only son, Louis Henry, b. in Fon Du Lac, August 31, 1865.

†VanRensalaer, m. Jane A. Skinner, November, 1850; is a farmer and resides at Boston, N. Y.

‡Richard L., m. Lucia A. Beecher, April 9, 1851; resides at Dunkirk, N. Y.; merchant and postmaster.

‖Talcott P., m. Elizabeth McRea, in California; resides at Knight's Ferry, California.

§Amzi B., m. Ellen Wade, October, 1856; was surgeon of 12th Wisconsin Regiment; d. in service.

(*a*)Eugene B., m. Martha Rowe, in Michigan, 1858; was Captain in a Wisconsin Regiment, 2 years; is a lawyer and resides at Nashville, Tenn.

His children were:

    I.   MARY, b. February 19, 1815.

    II.   DAMARIS, b. February 18, 1817.   m. —— Jones.

    III. FANNY, b. August 29, 1819.

    IV. TRUMAN, b. November 27, 1821.

    V.   ROXANIA, b. January 16, 1824.

    VI. DANFORD A., b. July 31, 1833. d. November 9,
          1868.

No. 176.

JOSEPH CARY, son of Asa, No. 85, b. in Williamsburg, Mass., December 27, 1797 ; m. Eliza Ayres, in Erie county, N. Y., October 5, 1823; removed to Freeport, Ills.; he d. December 8, 1870.

His children were:

    I.   WESLEY,* b. September 8, 1824.

    II.   ERASTUS,† b. September 28, 1828.

    III. WEALTHY,‡ b. May 16, 1839.

*WESLEY, m. Hannah N. Pass, December 13, 1853; has two sons and one daughter; in Freeport, Ills.

†ERASTUS, m. Priscilla Boenebright, December 10, 1852; has two sons and one daughter in Freeport, Ills.; he d. October 19, 1870.

‡WEALTHY, m. Austin S. Smith, October 2, 1862; lives in Webster City, Iowa.

No. 177.

Sylvester Cary, son of Asa, No. 85, b. in Cazenovia, N. Y., August 16, 1800; m. Cynthia Alverson, January 19, 1821; is a clergyman at Pine Lake, Michigan.

His children were:

I.   Amy,* b. April 28, 1822.

II.   Sylvester,† b. September 12, 1831.

No. 178.

Van Rensalaer Cary, son of Asa, No. 85, b. at Cazenovia, N. Y., January 5, 1805; m. Sophia Streeter, January 1, 1826, and removed to Freeport, Ills.

His children were:

I.   Sylvester, b. February 23, 1827.   No. 294.

II.   John W., b. March 5, 1829.   No. 295.

*Amy, m. Luman Fuller, of Milford, Mich., November 30, 1841; had seven children; d. April 24, 1853.

†Sylvester, m. Meta Waltets, at Kalamazoo, Mich.; had four children all of whom d. in infancy; he is living at Hawley Springs, Miss.

No. 179.

Asa Cary, son of Asa, No. 85, b. in Erie county, N.Y., August 22, 1821 ; m. Laura Rice, November 18, 1849 ; removed to Silver Creek, N. Y., where he now resides.

His children were:

    I.   Homer A., b. May 28, 1854.

    II.   Almira A., b. December 25, 1858.

    III.   Sibian G., b. March 12, 1861.

    IV.   Laura A., b. September 24, 1862.

    V.   Edgar H., b. September 27, 1864.

No. 180.

Ebenezer Cary, son of Ebenezer, No. 86, b. in Western New York, 1816 ; m. Catherine J. Fonda ; he d. November, 1863.

His children were:

    I.   Alfred, b. October 2, 1854.

    II.   Ebenezer, b. February 10, 1857.

    III.   Mary, b. March 28, 1859.

    IV.   John, b. October 26, 1861.

No. 181.

WALTER CARY, son of Trumbull, No. 87, b. in Batavia, N. Y., December 21, 1818 ; m. Julia Love, at Buffalo, April 14, 1848 ; was educated at Union College, N. Y.; studied medicine and stands high in his profession, at Buffalo, N. Y.

His children were :

I. TRUMBULL, b. August 1, 1849.

II. THOMAS, b. April 27, 1851.

III. CHARLES, b. October 20, 1852. At Harvard University.

IV. JENNIE, b. December 23, 1854.

V. WALTER, b. February 26, 1857

VI. GEORGE, b. March 25, 1859.

VII. LEWENA, b. January 1, 1862.

No. 182.

WALDO CARY, son of Ezekiel, No. 88, b. in Williman-tic, Ct., April 3, 1772 ; he was a shoemaker by trade, and lived for a time in Vermont, but returned to his native town and settled on the farm of his maternal ancestor ; his farm became very valuable on account of its proximity to the village. He was twice m., first, Fidelia, daughter of Dr. Nathan Arnold, of Mansfield, Ct., 1793, she d. in 1813 ; and he m. second, Freelove, daughter of Captain Michael F. Durant,, of New London, Ct., 1814.

His children were ;

I.   SOPHRONIA, b. October 14, 1794.   m. E. D. Fitch,
      of Willimantic, Ct.

II. JULIA, b. November 1, 1796.   d. 1813.

III. FIDELIA,* b. 1799.

IV. LUCRETIA, b. 1803.   m. C. York, of New York.

V.   EZEKIEL WALDO,† b. August 13, 1807.

VI. JULIA E., b. October 10, 1816.   m. Rev. Wil-
      liam Wright.

VII. DUMONT RIPLEY,‡ b. November, 1819.

No. 183.

JOHN CARY, son of William, No. 89, b. in Scotland, Ct.,
March 18, 1778 ; m. Sybil Gaser, 1810 ; he resided in Scotland, and d. 1854 ; his widow d. 1845.

His children were :

I.   FRANCES HARRIET,‖ b. 1811.

II. ALATHEA, b. 1813.   d. unm.

III. EDVIN WALES, b. 1815.   n. t.

IV. GILES, b. 1821.   n. t.

---

*FIDELIA, m. first Reuben Safford, second, David Douglass ; had sev-
eral children ; went to S. America, and d. there ; family reside in S. America.
    †EZEKIEL W., m. Harriet M. Field ; had one son, who d. in infancy.
He lives in Willimantic ; childless.
    ‡DUMONT R., m. and had one child ; both dead.
    ‖FRANCES H., m. B. P. Barrett ; lives in Killingly, Ct.; no issue.

No. 184.

ELIJAH CARY, son of William, No. 89, b. in Scotland, Ct., October 4, 1780; was a farmer; m. Tabitha Bushnell, of Lisbon, Ct., September 22, 1813; he d. September 22, 1845; his widow living in Scotland, in 1863.

His children were:

    I.   ESTHER BURNETT,* b. October 4, 1814.

    II.   ALFRED WILLIAM, b. July 24, 1819.   No. 296.

    III.   HENRY LORIN, b. November 21, 1824.   No. 297.

No. 185.

WILLIAM CARY, son of William, No. 89, b. in Scotland, Ct., December 10, 1782; he m. Lucinda Lillie, 1810; was a carpenter and farmer in Scotland; he d. in 1844; his widow removed to Illinois.

His children were;

    I.   THERON, b. December 16, 1810.   No. 298.

    II.   FREDERICK WILLIAM, b. June 6, 1813.   No. 299.

    III.   MARY L.,* b. December 12, 1814.

    IV.   HORACE, b. August 5, 1819.   No. 300.

    V.   HARRIET E.,† b. November 28, 1824.

    VI.   EDWIN AUGUSTUS, b. September 24, 1826. d. 1828.

    VII.   AUGUSTUS E., b. August 25, 1830.   In Illinois.

*ESTHER B., m. H. Mowry, of Bozrah, Ct., and moved to Brooklyn, N.Y.
*MARY L., m. George Bass and went to Illinois.
†HARRIET E., m. John Brown, and lives at St. Albans, Vt.

No. 186.

FREDERICK CARY, son of Jonathan, No. 90, b. in Norwich, Ct., 1786; m. Anna Savage, in Norwich, June 22, 1817; removed to Knox county, Ohio; settled on a farm where he resided in 1864; his wife d. November 13, 1863.

His children were·

    I.   THOMAS,* b. July 31, 1818.

   II.   EMILY,† b. August 8, 1820.

  III. WILLIAM L. b. September 25, 1822. No. 301.

  IV. CAROLINE, b. November 15, 1824. d. unm. December 2. 1863.

    V. GEORGE W.,‡ b. January 28, 1827.

  VI. FREDERICK WILLIAM, b. July 18, 1829. d. unm. January 2, 1853.

 VII. JOHN, b. January 22, 1832. d. unm. August 5, 1856.

VIII. CHARLES, b. March 10, 1834. unm.

  IX. JAMES, b. May 4, 1838. unm.

*THOMAS, m. Cynthia Merriman, September 8, 1853; resides in Knox county; has one daughter, b. March 18, 1855.

†EMILY, m. James Merriman, and resides at Mt. Gilead, Morrow Co.,O.

‡GEORGE W., m. Sarah Chambers, has no issue.

No. 187.

Ralph Cary, son of Jonathan, No. 90, b. in Norwich, Ct., 1789; m. Emily Smith, in Scotland, Ct., 1814; removed to Hartford, Ct., where he d. in 1860.

His children were:

    I.   Martha A., b. 1817. d. 1829.

    II.   Winthrop H., b. 1818. No. 302.

    III.   James S., b. 1820. No. 303.

    IV.   George B., b. 1823. No. 304.

    V.   William H., b. 1826. Went to California. n. t.

    VI.   Frederick A..* b. 1830.

    VII.   Martha E., b. 1837. d. 1841.

No. 188.

James Cary, son of Capt. James, No. 91, b. in Scotland, Ct., December 7, 1777; was a farmer and settled in Canterbury, Ct.; frequently represented the town in the legislature; filled many town offices; was honest and upright, kind and courteous, and highly respected. He m. Phebe, daughter of William Howard, October 25, 1804; he d. August 14, 1861, aged 84 years; his wife d. 1847, aged 69 years.

---

*Frederick A., m. Cordelia Church; resides in Hartford, Ct.; had one daughter, Emma L., b. 1861

His children were:

I,   PHEBE HOVARD,* b. December 17, 1805.

II.   ABIGAIL KINGSBURY,† b. August 22, 1807.

III.   JAMES BENEIJAH, b. August 22, 1810.   No. 305.

iV.   ANNA BRADFORD, b. February 9, 1815.   d. unm.
     May 7, 1841.

No. 189.

SANFORD CARY, son of Captain James, No. 91, b. in Scotland, Ct., July 14, 1784 ; m. Caroline, daughter of Jabez Tracy, May 16, 1811 ; was a respectable farmer in Scotland ; he d. May 2, 1852 ; .his wife d. May 3, 1861, aged 74 years.

His children were:

I.   HENRY HUDSON, b. July 2, 1814.   No. 306.

II.   DVIGHT, b. February 24, 1817.   No. 307.

III.   WOLCOTT, b. June 29, 1819.   No. 308.

IV.   JANE, b. September 8, 1823.   m. Nelson Morse.

No. 190.

HORATIO CARY, son of Anson, No. 93, b. in Chenango county, N. Y., March 27, 1785 ; m. Elizabeth Rhodes ; removed to Madison, Wisconsin, where his family still resides ; he d. February 10, 1855.

*PHEBE, m. Wm. F. Willoughby, October 15, 1827 ; and had a family of children.

†ABIGAIL, m. David F. Adams, of Canterbury, April 3, 1832.

I.   GEORGE A.   n. t.

II.   HORATIO G.   n. t.

III.   HENRY R.   n. t.

IV.   CHARLES P.   n. t.

V.   JOHN B.   n. t.

VI.   ALBERT G.   n. t.

VII.   EMELINE, m. —— Van Valkenburg, had two daughters, and d. at Lockport, N. Y.

No. 191.

GEORGE Λ. CARY, son of Anson, No. 93, b. in Chenango county, N. Y., May 8, 1793; m. first, Sarah Walters, March 29, 1820, she d. June 18, 1821; and second, Adeline E. Crandall, May 8, 1854; when last heard from he was still living in Oxford, N. Y.

His children were:

I.   SARAH W., b. 1821.   m. William N. Mason, and had two children.

No. 192.

PALMER C. CARY, son of Anson, No. 93, b. in Oxford, Chenango county, N. Y., March 31, 1798; m. Rowena Osgood, April 17, 1826, and resides in Oxford.

His children were:

I.   ANSON L.
II. LUCY. d. unm. at 20 years of age.
III. ROVENA. m. T. Walters.
IV. JANE M.
V.   FRANCES. m. F. Laguin, of Joliet, Ills. d. May 17, 1861, leaving two daughters.

No. 193.

ZALMON S. CARY, son of Anson, No. 93, b. at Oxford, Chenango county, N. Y., August 31, 1800; m. December 5, 1824; he d. August 23, 1854.

I.   HARRIET M.,* b. March 14, 1827.
II. SARAH ELIZABETH,† b. April 22, 1829.
III. HELEN M.,‡ b. March 10, 1832.
IV. MARY B., b. August 22, 1835.
V.   JOHN, b. October 25, 1837.

*HARRIET M., m. —— Bradley, of Wisconsin; had one child, and d. May 23, 1862.

†SARAH E., m. Stephen Roripaugh; had family and lived at New Bedford, Mass.

‡HELEN M., m. J. A. Wiswell, May 10, 1863; resides in Minnesota.

No. 194.

ROBERT CARY, son of Christopher, No. 94, b. in Lyme, N. H., January 24, 1787; went with his father to the North-west Territory, in 1802; lived for some years in Cincinnati, but settled on a farm, near College Hill, O.; was a soldier in the war of 1812, was with General Hull at the surrender. He was a quiet, unostentatious, upright man; lived and died highly respected by all who knew him; he d. November 13, 1866.

He m. Eliza Jessup, of Hamilton county, Ohio, in 1813, she d. of consumption, July 30, 1835.

His children were:

    I.   ROVENA,* b. October 18, 1814.

    II. SUSAN,† b. May 1, 1816.

    III. RHODA, b. 1818. d. 1833.

    IV. ALICE,‡ b. April 26, 1820.

*ROWENA, m. Isaac B. Carnahan, of Cincinnati; had several daughters of decided talent; she d. about 1868.

†SUSAN, m. Alex. Swift of Cincinnati; had one son and one daughter; she d. 1852; her son and daughter both died of consumption; the daughter, Alice Swift, was the especial favorite of her distinguished nieces, Alice and Phebe, and was the legatee of their personal effects; she m. George Clymer,; had two children; d. in Florida, February 14, 1873.

‡ALICE, was a poetess of world-wide fame, and authoress of several books; she d. in New York City, February 12, 1871. A memorial volume of Alice and her sister Phebe, by Mrs. Mary Clemmer Ames, has been published since the death of the sisters, together with volumes of their later poems.

V.   Asa,‖ b. May 5, 1822.

VI.   Phebe,§ b. September 4, 1824.

VII.   Warren,(*a*) b. October 16, 1826.

VIII.   Lucy, b. 1829.   d. 1833.

IX.   Elmina, (*b*) b. 1831.

No. 195.

Beneijah Cary, son of Christopher No. 94, b. in Lyme, N. H., 1788 : removed to Cincinnati, with father, in 1802 ; served in the war of 1812 ; m. Polly Nichols, of Hartford, Vt., in 1812 ; settled on a farm near College Hill, O., resided there many years and moved to a farm near New Richmond, O., where he d. 1858.

‖Asa, m. Leah A. Woodruff, 1850 ; had two sons, Absalom and Walter Scott, both of whom d. in infancy. He is a farmer and resides near College Hill, O.: a worthy, esteemed and useful citizen.

§Phebe, was an authoress and poetess little less celebrated than her sister, Alice ; they were inseperable companions ; she d. at Newport, R. I., July 31, 1871 ; the remains of Alice and Phebe, repose in Greenwood Cemetery, N. Y.

(*a*) Warren, is a respectable farmer near Harrison, Ohio ; has been twice married ; had two sons, Alexander and Robert ; Alexander was killed by an accident, January 1, 1866 ; Robert lives with his father.

(*b*) Elmina, m. Alexander Swift, and d. childless in 1862.

His children were :

I. MARIA,* b. 1813.

II. CHRISTOPHER,† b. 1816.

III. FRANCIS,‡ b. 1819.

IV. BENJAMIN F.,‖ b. 1821.

V. MARTHA, b. 1824. m. —— Hopper in Cincinnati, and d.

VI. MARY, b. 1827. m. Thomas Kenelly, had two daughters. d. 1855.

VII. AMANDA, b. 1828. d. 1837.

VIII. ADELINE, b. 1833. d. 1834.

IX. VARUS B.,§ b. 1835.

X. ANDREW JACKSON, ⎫ b. 1838. ⎰ d. 1839

XI. MARTIN VAN BUREN, ⎭ ⎱ (a)

XII. VENUS, b. 1841. d. 1841

No. 196.

IRVIN CARY, son of Christopher, No. 94, b. near Cincinnati, O., 1826; m. and removed to Missouri, where he still resides.

*MARIA, m. Gilbert Hathorn ; had several children ; lives in Minnesota.

†CHRISTOPHER, studied medicine; m. twice ; had one son and d. in Indiana.

‡FRANCIS, m. and has children ; lives at New Richmond, Ohio.

‖BENJAMIN F., m. and had three daughters, and d.

§VARUS B., m. Sarah Crawford ; had one son who d. in infancy ; he d. in the Union Army.

(a)MARTIN VAN B., d. in the Union Army in 1862, much beloved.

His children were :

   I.   CLINTON F., b. 1854.

   II.   DILLSWORTH, b. 1858.

No. 197.

ORRIN CARY, son of John, No. 95, b. at Hudson, N. Y. July 26, 1807; m. Margaret E. Stever, September 20, 1834; is a carpenter, and resides at Elizabeth Port, N. J.

His children were:

   I.   LORENZO J.,* b. March 26, 1836.

   II.   SARAH A., b. December 14, 1837.   m. Charles W. Brown. August 21, 1861.

   III.   ABRAM STEVER,† b. November 12, 1839.

   IV.   JOHN ERASTUS,‡ b. August 8, 1842.

   V.   WILLIAM WOODWARD,‖ b. August 12, 1847.

   VI.   FRANCES ELIZA,§ b. July 7, 1849.

*LORENZO J., m. Mary Haskins, March 6, 1865; lives at Preble, N. Y.

†ABRAM S., was a noble young man ; d. in the Union Army, at New Orleans, La., September 30, 1863.

†JOHN E., m. Maria D. Ball, January 2, 1868; was a brave soldier in the Union Army.

‖WILLIAM W., m. Rachel Donehue, March 16, 1870.

§FRANCES E., m. Alex. C. Henry, July 29, 1868 ; d. March 3, 1871.

No. 198.

Lorenzo Cary, son of John, No. 95, b. in Hudson, N. Y., 1813; graduated with honor at Yale College, in the class of 1835; became a Congregational minister and preached with great acceptance at Webster, Mass.; m. Sarah E. Peck, (a widow,) in 1838; was elected professor of languages in Farmer's College, O. in 1851; was a ripe scholar, an excellent preacher and a good and true man; he d. of apoplexy at College Hill, O., 1857.

His children were:

I.   Ferdinand E., b. 1840. unm. in Chicago, Ills.
II. Sarah Josephine, b. 1842. unm. in Chicago, Ills.
III. Anna Gertrude, b. 1844. unm. in Chicago, Ills.
IV. Samuel Fenton, b. 1846. d. in Union Army.

No. 199.

Freeman Grant Cary, son of William, No. 96. b. in Cincinnati, O., April 9, 1810; graduated at Miami University, in the class of 1831; devoted more than thirty years of his life to teaching; established an academy at College Hill, O., called "Cary's Academy;" was eminently successful as a teacher; originated the Farmer's College, and was president

for a number of years; the institution under his management
had three-hundred pupils; he was an enthusiast in horticul-
ture and agriculture; established and edited the "Cincin-
natus," an agricultural periodical of great merit.   After
spending thirty years in teaching, he retired to a farm in Butler county, O., devoting himself with great zeal and energy
to the practical application of his scientific knowledge; he
still resides on his elegant farm. He m. first, Malvina Macan,
April 4, 1833, she d. January, 1872; and second, Mrs. Jane
Richardson, March, 1873.

His children were:

    I. REBECCA FENTON,* b. March 5, 1834.

   II. ELIZABETH, b. April 29, 1836. d. September 20,
        1838.

  III. MARIA, b. March 15, 1836. d. February 12, 1840.

  IV. MALVINA ESTELLA,† b. January 13, 1841.

   V. ANNA RAMSAY,‡ b. February 16, 1844.

  VI. WILLIAM, b. March 7, 1847. unm.

 VII. SAMUEL FENTON, b. June 2, 1849. unm.

VIII. MARY, b. March 2, 1855. unm.

---

*REBECCA F., graduated at the Wesleyan Female College, Cincinnati, an
accomplished scholar; m. Dr. Wm. B. Ludlow; has two sons and two daughters; resides at Hamilton, O.

†MALVINA E., m. George Roll; has a family of children, and resides in
Auglaize county, Ohio.

‡ANNA R., graduated at Ohio Female College, a succesful teacher; m.
John Henderson, Esq., of Cleveland, Ohio.

No. 200.

WILLIAM WOODVARD CARY, son of William No. 96, b. in Cincinnati, O., February 23, 1812; pursued a scientific course at Miami University; was distinguished for his acquirements in mathematics; chose farming for his profession; settled on a portion of the paternal estate, at College Hill, O.; was a quiet, useful and honorable citizen; m. Eleanor Smith, of Poughkeepsie, N. Y., April 30, 1835. In the summer of 1845, he overworked himself, and produced a disease, from which he suffered intensely, until relieved by death, July 25, 1848. His wife d. of ship-fever, October 30, 1854, at Poughkeepsie, N. Y.; their daughter, Helen, d. at same place of same disease, October 25, 1854.

His children were:

I. HELEN M., b. June 11, 1836. d. October 25, 1854.

II. ADALYN S., b. December 9, 1838. unm.

III. EMILY IONE,* b. December 14, 1840.

IV. MARIA,† b. June 2, 1844.

---

*EMILY J., m. Alonzo Horton, September 27, 1860, and d. childless, September 11, 1863.

†MARIA, m. David Carnahan, September 19, 1861: had one son, William Woodward, who is still living; she d. November 12, 1867.

No. 201.

SAMUEL FENTON CARY, son of William, No. 96, b. at Cincinnati, O., February 18, 1814; graduated at Miami University, in the class of 1835; studied law and graduated at the Cincinnati Law College, in 1837; practiced the profession in Cincinnati, until 1844, when he abandoned the profession to devote his time and energies to the promotion of the temperanee reform; he lectured in all parts of twenty-seven states, all the British Provinces of North America, and in all the leading cities and towns of England, Ireland, Scotland and Wales. He edited several papers and magazines; was elected to the chief-office of the Sons of Temperance, in North America, at Baltimore, Md., in 1847. He had some celebrity as a political speaker, and was elected to the Fortieth Congress, from the Second Ohio District. He resides at College Hill, Ohio, and in January, 1873, returned to the practice of law, in Cincinnati, O.

For several years he devoted leisure hours in gathering up the memorials of the Cary Family, and this printed volume is the result.

He was twice m., first to Maria Louisa Allen, October 18, 1836, she d. of consumption, September 25, 1847; and he m. second, Lida S., daughter of J. G. Stillwell, Esq., May 29, 1849.

His children were:

I.   MARTHA LOUISA,* b. September 16, 1837.

II. ELLA WOODNUTT, b. February 13, 1841. m. Edward Sayre, 1871.

III. LOU ALLEN, b. May 24, 1847. d. July 4, 1847.

IV. OLIVE, b. August 12, 1851. d. September 19, 1852.

V.   SAMUEL FENTON, b. March 22, 1857.

VI. JESSIE, b. October 13, 1858.

No. 202.

JOSIAH CARY, son of Josiah, No. 87, b. in Haddam, Ct., June 23, 1791; m. Eunice Tripp, December 25, 1817.

*MARTHA, m. Charles B. Huber; had a son, Charles Woodnutt, b. April 2, 1856; she d. of consumption, December 16, 1856.

His children were;

   I.   Anna M., b. October 20, 1818. m. Edwin E. Anable.

   II.   Clark S., b. February 2, 1821. d. in infancy.

   III.   Jonathan T., b. March 31, 1823. No. 309.

   IV.   Clark W., b. January 28, 1825. No. 310.

   V.   Lydia, b. March 28, 1827. m. James M. Newton, October 21, 1844.

   VI.   Mary J., d. December 19, 1830. m. Myron H. Peck, July 7, 1853.

   VII.   Jedediah T., b. February 13, 1833. No. 311.

   VIII.   Benjamin H., b. January 26, 1835. No. 312.

Seventh Generation.

No. 203.

Eleazer Cary, son of Eleazer, No. 99, b. in Windham, Ct., 1811 ; was a carpenter in Willimantic, Ct.; went to sea ; d. at sea. 1850.

His children were :

    I.   Lucius Henry, b. 1838.   Sea Captain.

    II.   Imogene, b. 1840. d. 1855.

    III.   Lydia, b. 1842. d. 1859.

    IV.   George Thomas, b. 1843. d. 1860.

    V.   Julian, b. 1845. d. in Union Army.

No. 204.

WILLIAM ADDISON CARY, son of William, No. 102, b.
in ~~Amesbury, Mass.,~~ *Lempster N.H.* July 23, 1818; m. Lydia Gould, of
Northfield, and lives at Malden, Mass.

His children were:

   I.   EMMA AUGUSTA, b. 1840.

   II. ANNA MARIA, b. 1842. d. 1844.

  III. ANN SOPHIA, b. 1846. d. 1847.

  IV. MARY ALICE, b. 1849.

   V. HARRIET, b. 1850. d. 1854.

  VI. WINNIFRED, b. 1855.

 VII. WILLIAM ADDISON, b. 1856.

No. 205.

MILAN GALUSHA CARY, son of William, No. 102, b. in
~~Amesbury, Mass.,~~ *Lempster N.H.* November 20, 1823; m. ~~Mary~~ *Emily* Denett,
1847; he d. at Medford, Mass., 1854.

His children were:

   I. THESTA SOPHIA, b. 1848.

  II. HENRY FRANK, b. 1851.

No. 206.

AUGUSTUS CELAN_{us}, son of William, No. 102, b. in ~~Ames-bury, Mass.~~, September 16, 1825 ; m. Harriet E. Folsom, 1846, at Amesbury.

His children were :

    I.   WILLIAM AUGUSTUS, b. 1848.

    II. GEORGE ROSVELL, b. 1850.

    III. ANNIE SUSAN. b. 1853.

    IV. NELLIE LEE, b. 1856.

No. 207.

JOSEPH CARY, son of Samuel, No. 106, b. in Albany county, N. Y., January 30, 1802 ; m. Lydia, daughter of Cornelius Chase, of Cheatham, N. Y., 1825; is a worthy member of the Society of Friends. and highly respected by all who know him ; resides at Albany, N. Y.

His children were:

I.   MARY ANN, ·b. 1826.
II. LUCIA, b. 1828. m. George Brown, of Brook-
     lyn, N. Y., 1852.
III. ELIZABETH, b. 1829. d. 1831.
IV. ELIZA, b. 1833.
V.   ALBERT, b. 1835. m. Emma Server, in 1859, in
     Albany, N, Y.
VI. MARIAH, b. 1837.
VII. EDVARD, } b. 1840. {
VIII. EGBERT } { m. Amelia Wolford, 1861.
     Lives in Albany, N. Y.

No. 208.

ISAAC H. CARY, son of Samuel, No. 106, b. in Albany
county, N. Y., May 7, 1812 ; m. Emily Hyde, of Rensalaerville, N. Y., 1844 ; a worthy member of the Society of Friends
in Albany, N. Y.

His children were:

I.   EDVIN H., b. 1846.

No. 209.

GEORGE CARY, son of Samuel, No. 106, b. in Albany county, N. Y., November 30, 1814 ; m. Caroline, daughter of Nathaniel Sawyer, 1842 ; is a worthy member of the Society of Friends, in Albany, N. Y.

His children were :
I.   ELIZABETH, b. 1843.
II. GEORGE, b. 1848. d. 1848.
III. JOSEPH ALBERT, b. 1852.

No. 210.

HON. JEREMIAH E. CARY, son of Joseph, No. 107, b. in Coventry, R. I.. April 30, 1803·; removed to Cherry Valley, N. Y.; m. Mary E., daughter of James Brackett, Esq.; is a lawyer by profession ; was a member of Congress and now lives at Brooklyn, N. Y., practicing law in New York City ; a quiet, but man of high character.

His children were :

 I. MARY E., b. 1831. m. George M. Allen, Brockport, N. Y.

 II. JOHN ELY, b. 1833. Surgeon in the Army.

 III. MARGARET LOUISA, b. 1835. m. Frederick Van
   Hitch, New York City.

 IV. ELIZA M., b. 1837.

 V. WILLIAM B., b. 1841. Was First Lieutenant
   New York Cavalry.

 VI. JOSEPH L., b. 1843.

 VII. CHARLES A., b. 1845.

 VIII. ANNA EATON, b. 1849.

 IX. HELEN IDA, b. 1851.

 X. CATHERINE A., b. 1854.

No. 211.

ALFRED X. CARY, son of Joseph, No. 107, b. in Coventry, R. I., March 28, 1811 ; m. Sarah Musdirk, 1833 ; removed
to Brockport, N. Y., and thence to Grand Rapids, Mich.,
where he now resides, a merchant.

His children were :

 I. SARAH JANE, b. 1835. d. 1843.

 II. ELIZABETH D., b. 1836. m. Robert M. Collins.

 III. CHARLES HENRY,* b. 1838.

*CHARLES HENRY, was First Lieutenant; in the Signal Corps ; d. in
the service, in Mississippi, July, 1863.

No. 212.

Josiah Whitney Cary, son of Darius H., No. 108, b. at Richfield, N. Y., 1808 ; m. —— Ward, in Rochester, N. Y , 1835 . d. at Albany, N. Y., 1842.

His children were :
  I.   Henry W., b. 1836. d. 1836.
  II.   Emeline, b. 1838. d. 1839.
  III.   Louisa E., b. 1840. Living in Ontario Co., N.Y.
  IV.   Calista, b. 1842. d. 1843.

No. 213.

Edwin Cary, son of Darius H., No. 108, b. at Richfield, N. Y., 1817 ; m. Adelia M. Gaige, 1849 ; resides in Richfield.

His children were :
  I.   Fanny, b. 1850.
  II.   Rhoda, b. 1851. d. 1852.
  III.   Martha J., b. 1853.

No. 214.

Joseph Cary, son of William, No. 109, b. in Herkimer county, N. Y.; m. Caroline Eames, 1840; removed to and resides in Milwaukee, Wisconsin.

His children were:

    I.   William Henry, b. 1841.

    II.   Charles Joseph, b. 1843.

    III.   Edward Lester, b. 1846.

    IV.   Caroline Eames. b. 1850.

No. 215.

William Hutchins Cary, son of William, No. 109, b. in Herkimer county, N. Y., 1816; m. Mary B. Taylor, of Milwaukee, Wisconsin, 1853; removed to and resides in Hastings, Minnesota.

His children were:

    I.   George Hutchins, b. 1854.

    II.   Frederick Willaim, b. 1857.

    III.   Walter, b. 1859.

No. 216.

GEORGE W. CARY, son of William, No. 109, b. in Herkimer county, N. Y., 1819; m. Sarah Ann Dickson, of Paris, N. Y., 1846: he d. 1850; his family reside at Fly Creek, Ostego county, N. Y.

His children were:

   I. ANN ELIZABETH, b. 1847.

   II. ALFRED D., b. 1849,

No. 217.

EBENEZER CARY, son of Dr. William, No. 111, b. in Saratoga county, N. Y.; November 5, 1797; m. and lived in Saratoga county; d· in Warren county, N. Y.,

His children were:

   I. MARIA, b. April 24, 1821. d. unm. March 19, 1845.

   II. AMY, b. April 23, 1826.

   III. LYDIA, b. February 2, 1828.

   IV. MARY, b. July 5, 1829.

   V. SAMUEL, b. April 9. 1831. d. December 23, 1859.

   VI. RUTH, b. April 25, 1838. d. July 2, 1860.

No. 218.

Lucius Cary, son of Dr. William, No. 111, b. in Saratoga county, N. Y., May 9, 1799; m. and lived and d. at Moreau, Saratoga county, N. Y.

His children were:

    I.   Ruth, b. August 1, 1821.

    II.   Joseph, b. April 30, 1823.

    III.   Mary A., b. March 5, 1827.

    IV.   Egbert, b. November 11, 1828.

    V.   James R., b. October 13, 1831.

    VI.   Matilda, b. August 11, 1833. d. April 7, 1863.

    VII.   John M., b. April 21, 1835. d. May 30, 1861.

    VIII.   Kezia, b. June 16, 1837.

    IX.   William, b. May 17, 1839.

    X.   Lucius, b. May 21, 1841. d. in infancy.

    XI.   Cynthia, b. December 4, 1843.

No. 219.

Jarvis Cary, son of Dr. William, No. 111, b. in Saratoga county, N. Y., May 23, 1801 ; m. lived and d. in Wayne county, N. Y.

His children were;

    I.   John M., b. May 26, 1827.

    II.   Joseph W., b. December 16, 1828. d. October 9, 1860.

No. 220.

Isaac Cary, son of Dr. William, No. 111, b. in Saratoga county, N. Y., January 15, 1818; m. and resides at Half Moon, Saratoga county, N. Y.

His children were:

I.   Hannah C., b. January 8, 1857.

II. Charles, b. June 16, 1860.

III. William, b. September 13, 1862.

No. 221.

William Cary, son of Taylor, No. 112, b. in Saratoga county, N. Y., July 12, 1803; m. Celesta Gridley, April 7, 1831; is a respectable farmer in Sheridan, Chatauque county, N. Y.

His children were:

I. Celesta, b. March 29, 1835.   d. in infancy.

II. Maria, b. December 19, 1839.   unm.

No. 222.

JOHN M. CARY, son of Taylor, No. 112, b. in Oneida county, N. Y.; m. first, Fanny Hopkins, April 20, 1833, she d. May 26, 1864, aged 51 years; and he m. second, Louisa M. Baldwin, November 24, 1864; removed to Hamilton county, O., thence to Adrian, Mich., where he resides, an intelligent and respected farmer.

His children were:

I. ELIZABETH, b. September 4, 1835. m. B. F. Lathem, 1855.

II. IRA H.,* b. January 3, 1838.

III. MINERVA,
IV. WILLIAM H. } b. July 28, 1844. { d. Feb. 10, 1845.

V. LEVI J., b. May 24, 1849. d. December 2, 1849.

VI. FANNY JANE, b. b. March 17, 1851.

VII. BESSIE M., b. September 6, 1870.

---

*IRA H., m. Elizabeth Logan, at Montgomery. Hamilton county, Ohio, August 19, 1870.

No. 223.

Ebenezer Cary, son of Egbert, No. 113, b. in Beekman N. Y., 1822; m. Mary E. Degroff, 1844, and resides at Poughkeepsie, N. Y.

His children were:

I.   Egbert J., b. 1847.
II. Harriet E., b. 1848.
III. Sophia W., b. 1850. d. 1851.
IV. Lauetta C., b. 1856.
V.   Mary E., b. 1860.

No. 224.

Solomon Flagler Cary, son of Sturgis, No. 114, b. in Binghampton, N. Y., October 9, 1820; m. Sarah M. Jarvis, 1852, and resides in Binghampton, N. Y.

His children were:

I. William Ely, b. 1852.
II. Marietta J., b. 1855.

No. 225.

OLIVER A. CARY, son of Sturgis, No. 114, b. in Bing-hampton, N. Y., June 5, 1827; m. first, Sarah M. Newell, 1850, she d.; and he m. Virginia D. Hart, May 7, 1872, at Corning, N. Y.

His children were:

I.   CORNELIA M., b. 1852.
II. TRACY M., b. 1854.
III. EDVARD, b. 1855.
IV. MYRA SOMERS, b. October 4, 1873.

No. 226.

JOHN W. CARY, son of Cephas, No. 119, b. in Shelby county, O., January 3, 1805; m. —— Kenard, and resides in Sidney, O., a man in high esteem.

His children were :

I. ELIZABETH M., b. 1827. m. 1859. Resides in Sidney, Ohio.

II. CLARA B., b. 1829. m. 1854. Resides in Sidney, Ohio.

III. HATTIE R., b. 1833. m. 1857. Resides in Sidney, Ohio.

IV. ANNA K., b. 1835. m. 1855. Lives in Sidney, O.

V. JOHN W., b, 1837. d. 1839.

VI. B. FRANKLIN, b. 1842. m. and lives in Sidney, O.

VII. JANE, b. 1843. d. 1843.

VIII. EDVARD, b. 1846.

IX. JOHN S., b. 1848.

X. ELLA, b. 1851.

XI. JOHN W., b. 1853. d. 1858.

XII. TOM CORWIN, b. 1860.

No. 227.

WILLIAM A. CARY, son of Cephas, No. 119, b. at Sidney, Ohio, January 9. 1805 ; m. —— Vandemark.

His children were:

    I.   CATHERINE J., b. 1835.   Living near Sidney, O.

   II.   WILLIAM T., b. 1837.

  III.   HENRY CLAY, b. 1840.

  IV.   JOSEPHINE, b. 1844.

   V.   CLEMENTINE, b. 1848.

No. 228.

DAVID M. CARY, son of Cephas, No. 119, b. in Shelby county, Ohio, January 22, 1810; m. Isabella Gerard, January 22, 1832.

His children were:

    I.   CEPHAS S., b. November 25, 1832.

   II.   WILLIAM C., b. July 22, 1834.

  III.   GEORGE W.,
                 } b. and d. August 8, 1836.
  IV.   T. J.,

   V.   FINLEY W.,
                 } b. July 25, 1838.
  VI.   ALENA A.,

 VII.   CELESTINA C., b. May 1, 1841.   m. James B. Beach.

VIII.   MARY E., b. April 1, 1843.   d. December 19, 1843.

IX. RHODA J., b. December 1, 1845.

X. HESTER C., b. September 1, 1847.   d. October 29, 1851.

XI. DAVID A., b, September 1, 1849.

XII. CLARA S., b. December 1, 1851.

XIII. JULIA M., b. July 1, 1857.

No. 229.

THOMAS M. CARY, son of Cephas, No. 119, b. at Sidney, Ohio, December 16, 1812 ; m. —— Cole, and resided in Sidney, O.; d. 1873.

His children were :

I. MARCELLUS, b. 1831.

II. JOHN W., b. 1833.

III. STEPHEN, b. 1836. d. 1838.

IV. JOHN N., b. 1838.

V. LORETTA, b. 1841.

VI. TAMAR ANN, b. 1843.

VII. HARRY G., b. 1846.

VIII. NANCY A., b. 1852.

IX. WILLIAM T., b. 1856.

X. IDA M., b. 1857.

XI. —— }
XII. —— } d. in infancy.

No. 230.

JEREMIAH CARY, son of Cephas, No. 119, b. at Sidney, Ohio, June 7, 1814; m. and resides at Sidney, O.

His children were :

    I.   SARAH J. b. 1838. d. 1859.

   II.   DAVID R., b. 1840. d. 1840.

  III.   ELMORE Y., b. 1847. d. 1850.

  IV.   JOHN H., b. 1850. d. 1850.

   V.   FLORA H., b. 1853.

  VI.   MARY A,. b. 1861.

 VII.   LIZZIE T., b. 1863.

No. 231.

BENJAMIN WESLEY CARY, son of Cephas, No. 119, b. at Sidney, Ohio, October 1, 1816; m. —— Cole, and lives at Sidney, O.

His children were:

    I.   WILLIAM RAPER, b. 1838.

   II.   STEPHEN H., b. 1841.

  III.   LAURA CAROLINE, b. 1843.

  IV.   JANE WESLEY, b. 1850.

No. 232.

Simeon B. Cary, son of Cephas, No. 119, b. at Sidney, Ohio, December 30, 1823 ; m. and lives at Brooklyn, N. Y.

His children were :
I.   Ida F., b. May 3, 1857.   d. May 25, 1857.
II. Nellie, b. July 14, 1859.   d. October 26, 1859.
III. Jennie, b. October 15, 1860.
IV. Samuel C., b. December 16, 1861.

No. 233.

Harvey G. Cary, son of Cephas, No. 119, b. at Sidney, Ohio, August 18, 1826 ; m. Miss Newman, and resides in Indianapolis, Ind.; a man widely known and much esteemed.

His children were :
I.   Gertrude N., b. 1851.
II. John Newman, b. 1853.
III. Peter Love, b. 1856.

No. 234.

MILTON T. CARY, son of Cephas, No. 119, b. at Sidney, Ohio, July 22, 1831 ; studied medicine, was a surgeon in the Union Army ; resides in Cincinnati ; has a large practice, and stands high in his profession ; he m. Cornelia Burnett, 1856.

His children were :

I.   BURNETT, b. October 21, 1856. d. April 4, 1859.
II. MOLLIE, b. May 8, 1860.
III. LYDIA K., b. March 26, 1862.

No. 235.

HENRY SHORER CARY, son of George, No. 120, b. in Shelby county, Ohio, June 8, 1816; m. Margaret Ewing Chapman, September 28, 1837, in Union county, Ohio ; remained some time in Shelby and Champaign counties, Ohio ; removed to Lewis, Cass county, Iowa, 1848, where he d. September 16, 1867 ; his widow still lives in Lewis, Iowa.

His children were:

I.   SOPHIA AURORA, b. August 30, 1839.

II.   MARY BARBARA, b April 12, 1842.

III.   ELLENA ARADELIA. b. June 14, 1844.

IV.   SARADA, b. February 16, 1846.

V.   HUGH THOMPSON, b. September 14, 1847.

VI.   JOHN CALVIN WILLIAMSON, b. December 31, 1848. Lives in Des Moines, Iowa.

VII.   CLARA BELL. b. March 15, 1851.

VIII.   CHARLES HENRY WARDEN, b. July 10, 1854.

IX.   DAVID CHAPMAN, }
X.   GEORGE THOMPSON, } b. October 2, 1856.

XI.   CARRIE EUGENIA, b. September 8, 1859.

No. 236.

EZRA CARY, son of Thomas, No. 121, b. at Enfield, Mass., 1803; m. Lucretia P. Jenny, 1832; resides in Enfield, Mass.

His children were:

I.   THOMAS, b. 1833. d. unm.

II.   AURELIA, b. 1835.

III.   LUCRETIA, b. 1837.

No. 237.

EDVARD CARY, son of Thomas, No. 121, b. in Enfield, Mass., 1809; m. Elizia Tucker.

His children were:

    I.   CHARLES.   n. t.

    II.   HARVEY,   n. t.

    III.   GEORGE.   n. t.

    IV.   RUFUS.   n. t.

No. 238.

RUFUS CARY, son of Thomas, No. 121, b. in Enfield, Mass., 1813; m. and settled at Princeton, Ills.; a banker.

His children were:

    I.   FRANCIS.   n. t.

    II.   AURELIA,   n. t.

    III.   WARREN.   n. t.

No. 239.

ZACHARY CARY, son of Zachary, No. 122, b. at Sterling, Mass.; m. Miriam Morse, 1823, and resides in Norway, Oxford county, Me.

His children were:

I.   JAMES HENRY, b. 1824.   d. at Portland, Me., 1851.

II.   ALBERT QUINCY,* b. 1826.

III.   LYDIA ANN, b. 1829. d. 1829.

IV.   MARTHA JANE, b. 1832. m. W. B. Harman.

V.   GEORGE FRANCIS, b. 1837. m. Harriet N. Flood, 1866.

VI.   LEVIS CLARK, b. 1843.

No. 240.

THOMAS CARY, son of Zachary, No. 122, b. in Sterling, Mass., 1807; m. first. Miss Walker, in 1834; and second, Miss Waterhouse, in 1838; lives in Gray, Me.

---

*ALBERT QUINCY, was killed by the blowing up of the Steamer Princess, on the Mississippi river, 1859.

His children were:

   I.   SARAH C., b. 1835.

  II. THEDA, b. 1841

 III. CEPHAS, b. 1843.

 IV. GUSTAVUS, b. 1845.

  V. CYNTHIA, b. 1851.

No. 241.

SALMON CARY, son of Ezra, No. 123, b. in Turner, Me.,
1804; m. Anna Turner, in 1830: resides in Turner, Me.

His children were:

   I.   LORANA F., b. 1832. m. Frank Whitman, 1860.

  II. LOIS STAPLES, b. 1834. d. in infancy.

 III. THOMAS, b. 1836. Was in the Union Army.

 IV. SUSANNA D., b. 1838. d. in infancy.

  V. LYDIA A., b. 1841. d. in infancy.

 VI. SALMON W., b. 1843.

 VII. EZRA D., b. 1848.

No. 242.

SETH CARY, son of Ezra, No. 123, b. in Turner, Me., 1805; m. Susanna Hildreth, 1832; resided in Topsham Me.; d. 1857.

His children were:

- I. GEORGE, ⎫
- II. HENRY, ⎬ b. 1833.
- III. FRANCIS.
- IV. SAMUEL.
- V. HOSEA.
- VI. SUSANNA.
- VII. PRISCILLA. d. 1861.
- VIII. FRANCIS JANE. d. 1862.
- IX. MARVETTE.
- X. LUCY.

No. 243.

DANIEL CARY, son of Ezra, No. 123, b. in Turner, Me., 1806; m. Temperance Waterman, 1833: resides in Maine.

His children were :

I. AUGUSTUS, b. 1834.

II. ELLEN. b. 1836.   m. Augustus Carter, 1855.

III. LOIS AMELIA, b. 1841.

IV. DANIEL FREDERICK, b. 1848.   d. 1849.

V. HERBERT, b. 1851   d. 1853.

VI. CLARA ISABELLA, b. 1854.

No. 244.

WILLIAM R. CARY, son of Bethuel. No. 125, b. in Sumner, Me., 1820 ; m. Mary B. Clark, 1841 ; resides in East Sumner.

His children were :

I. SARAH, b. 1844.

II. MARY E., b. 1852.

III. LYDIA, b. 1856.

No. 245.

BENJAMIN F. CARY, son of Bethuel, No. 125, b. in Sumner, Me., 1822; m. Sophia Robinson, 1846.

His children were:

I.   BETHUEL, b. 1852.

II. LEONARD, b. 1860.

No. 246.

CHARLES CARY, son of Francis, No. 126, b. in Turner, Me., 1814; m. Sallie Bradford, 1837, and lives in Turner.

His children were:

I.   CHARLES KNOVLTON, b. December 26, 1838; m. Florence E. Potter, September 26, 1866, and resides in Boston, Mass.

II. MARY B., b. September 27, 1840.   m. Wallace Clark, Esq.

No. 247.

FRANCIS CARY, son of Francis, No. 126, b. in Turner, Me., 1824; m. Lois Allen, 1851, and resides in Turner.

His children were:

I. DANIEL, b. 1854.

No. 248.

LUTHER CARY, son of Cassander, No. 127, b. in Turner, Me., December 1, 1820; m. Dora Spencer, 1852.

His children were:

I. SARAH, b. 1856.

II. CLARA, b. 1861.

No. 249.

HARRISON GRAY OTIS CARY, son of Anslem, No. 129, b. in Greene, Me., December 28, 1816; removed with his parents to Zanesville, Ohio; m. Emma V. Bateman, October 13, 1842, she d. April 27, 1847; and he m. second; Matilda A. Ingalls, November 16, 1854. He is a druggist, residing at Zanesville, Ohio, the proprietor of a number of popular and celebrated prescriptions; an active and zealous philanthropist and christian.

His children were:

   I.   ELIZABETH COX, b. 1843, d. in infancy.

   II.   EDWARD RUSSELL,* b. January 2, 1845.

  III.   EMMA, b. April 10, 1847. d. September 8, 1847.

No. 250.

JARIUS CARY, son of Hugh, No. 131, b. in Turner, Me., September 25, 1823 ; m. Sophronia M. Foster, 1848, and lives in Turner, Maine.

His children were;

   I.   JULIA F., b. 1850.

   II.   EDVARD F., b. 1855.

  III.   ADA G., b. 1861.

*EDWARD R., resides at Des Moines, Iowa ; druggist by occupation.

No. 251.

SHEPPARD CARY, son of William H., No. 133, b. in
Holton, Maine, July 3, 1805 ; settled in Holton; was extensively engaged in trading, farming, etc.; was a prominent and
influential citizen: often in the legislature and in congress;
he m. Susanna Whittaker, at New Salem, Mass., December
25, 1832.

His children were :

    I.   THEODORE,* b. April 9, 1835.

    II. GEORGE, b. August 29, 1837.

    III. JEFFERSON, b. September 4, 1841.

    IV. JOHN H., ⎫ b. July 18, ⎰ d. September 19, 1845.

    V.   BION B., ⎭   1844. ⎱ d. April 1847.

No. 252.

WILLIAM HOLMAN CARY, son of William H., No. 133,
b. in Holton, Maine, October 23, 1812 ; m. first, Cordelia
Mathers, 1844, she d. April 29, 1849; and second, Adelaide
E. Cary, November, 1858.

*THEODORE, was editor and proprietor of the Aroostock Times, in
Houston, Maine.

His children were:

I. SYLVESTER, b. January 8, 1845.

II. WILLIAM H., b. April 2, 1849.

III. CATHERINE H., b. May 15, 1860.

IV. ANNIE A., b. November 25, 1861. d. January, 1862.

No. 253.

HORACE CARY, son of Ephraim, No. 134, b. at Minot, Maine, 1811 ; m. Miss Bradford, of Turner, Me., 1835.

His children were:

I. CHARLES, b. 1836. d. 1859.

II. ZOE JANE, b. 1839. m. H. Haskell, 1863.

III. LUCIUS, b. 1843.

IV. LYMAN, b. 1847.

No. 254.

Daniel Morris Cary, son of Joseph, No. 135, b. in Knox county, Ohio, June 17, 1806; m. Dorcas Rice, December 28, 1830; removed to Millersburg, Iowa.

His children were:

    I.   Sarah W., b. October 27, 1831. m. A. Ackers, 1855. d. July 7, 1856.

    II. William,* b. February 2, 1833.

    III. James B.,† b. June 24, 1835.

    IV. John A.,‡ b. May 24, 1838.

    V. Samuel P.,§ b. May 18, 1840.

    VI. Martha, b. February 11, 1843. m. Dr. J. S. Gaines, June, 1862.

    VII. Alvah A., b. November 17, 1845.

    VIII. Emily J., b. August 2, 1852. m. Allen Thompson, August 19, 1872.

*William, m. and resides in Millersburg, Iowa; has two sons, viz.: Wilford P., b. June 23, 1867; and Walter E., b. September 25, 1873.

†James B., m. Clara E. Penn, of Millersburg, Iowa, May 14, 1867; resides at Victor, Iowa; has one son, James H., b. August 2, 1868.

‡John A., belonged to 28th Iowa Regiment; m. Ellen C. Sherwood, June 23, 1861; had I. Charles A., b. June, 1862. II. Samuel D., b. January 13, 1869. III. Sherman G., b. December 8, 1873.

§Samuel P., m. Sarah B. Young. June 28, 1863; resides at Fort Des Moines, Iowa; had one daughter, Alice, b. April 18, 1864. He d. February 20, 1866.

No. 255.

ABEL CARY, son of Lewis, No. 137, b. in Ohio, October 2, 1809; studied medicine; settled in Salem, Columbiana county, Ohio; stood high as a man and as a physician. m. Maria P. Miller, May 5, 1843.

His children were:

    I.   ISABELLA, d. June 20, 1844. d. August. 15, 1845.

    II.   ASHBEL, b. January 6, 1846.

    III. BARCLAY, b. March 20, 1847. d. August 23, 1848.

    IV. DAVID M., b. January 26, 1849.

    V.   JAMES R., b. April 17, 1851.

    VI. CHARLES M., b. May 14, 1853.

    VII. LEVIS, b. May 14, 1855. d. January 8, 1857.

    VIII. ALICE, b. September 17, 1857.

    IX. WILLIAM B., b. December 9, 1860.

No. 256.

AARON CARY, son of Lewis, No. 137, b. in Ohio, August 17, 1813; m. Nancy Myers, of Bucyrus, Ohio, September 22, 1840; lives at Defiance, Ohio.

His children were:

    I.   LEVIS M., b. October 7, 1841.   m. Mattie C.
        Scott.

    II. MELANCHTON, b. May 21, 1844.

    III. ABRAM M., b. December 15, 1846.

    IV. WILLIAM H., b. June 14, 1850.

No. 257.

EDMUND CARY, son of Lewis, No. 137, b. in Ohio, October 27, 1815; m. Deliah Bartlett, October 27, 1840; removed to and resides at Rockton, Illinois.

His children were:

    I.   SARAH, b. October 12, 1841.   d. June 11, 1850.

    II.   PERMELIA, b. November 10, 1843.   d. December
         29, 1844.

    III. DANIEL B., b. April 8, 1845.   d. in the Union
         Army, March 19, 1864.

    IV. THOMAS J., b. August 27, 1847.

    V.   LUCRETIA, b. March 29, 1850.

    VI. ESTHER, b. January 29, 1852.

    VII. CHARLES W., b. July 8, 1854.

   VIII. KATE M., b. March 4, 1856.

    IX. SUSAN B., b. December 30, 1857.

    X.   GEORGE E., b. February 25, 1864.

No. 258.

GEORGE CARY, son of Lewis, No. 137, b, in Ohio, August 4, 1821; m. Catherine G. Gordon, April 10, 1849; removed to and resides at Beloit, Wisconsin.

His children were:

I.   HARRIET M., b. April 10, 1850. d. September 9, 1850.
II. LEVIS A., b. September 24, 1852.
III. GEORGE, b. August 4, 1855.
IV. JAMES C., b. October 4, 1857. d. May 12, 1859.
V.   PARVIN W., b. September 28, 1859, d. April 9, 1862.

No. 259.

LEVIS HENRY CARY, son of John, No. 139, b. in Morrow county, Ohio, March 27, 1813; m. Martha Chamberlain, January 8, 1839; removed to Toledo, Tamar county, Iowa, where he still resides.

His children were :

I. ——— a son, b. and d. February 8, 1840.

II. WILLIAM P., b. January 17, 1841. d. December 30, 1842.

III. JOHN LEVIS, b. February 24, 1843.

IV. MARY E., b. February 28, 1845.

V. LOU, b. April 29, 1848. d. May 2, 1848.

VI. MARTHA M., b. September 9, 1849.

VII. LUCRETIA A., b. November 18, 1852.

No. 260.

WILLIAM SNOOK CARY, son of John, No. 139, b. in Morrow county, Ohio, May 16, 1818 ; m. Mary A Gordon, February 21, 1843 ; removed to Alvorado, Steuben county, Indiana, where he resides.

His children were :

I. MARY ANN, b. January 18, 1844. m. Wm. H. Keys, January 18, 1865.

II. LAURANA, b. January 29, 1847. d. October 2, 1853.

III. MARGARET J., b. October 20, 1849. d. September 1, 1853.

    IV.   Levinna E., b. November 11, 1851. d. August 20, 1853.

    V.   William G., b. October 9, 1854.

    VI.   John L., b. March 28, 1858.

    VII.   Nelson E., b. November 29, 1861.

No. 261.

John R. Cary, son of John, No. 139, b. in Morrow county, Ohio, August 7, 1826; m. Eliza S. Lewis, July 1, 1845; removed to and resides in Garden Grove, Decatur county, Iowa; is a minister of the M. E. Church.

His children were:

    I.   Edvard G,, b. July 5, 1846.

    II.   Leonard B., b. June 26, 1848.

    III.   Emma, b. January 25, 1851.

    IV.   John Levis, b. May 18, 1854.

    V.   Alice B., b. March 4, 1857.

    VI.   Clara B., b. April 3, 1859.

No. 262.

GEORGE C. CARY, son of John, No. 139, b. in Morrow county, Ohio. March 20, 1823; m. Cordelia Purvis, December 31, 1849; removed to and resides at Alvorado, Steuben county, Indiana.

His children were:

I.   WILLARD P., b. October 10, 1850.   d. November 9, 1851.

II. LEVIS W., b. September 14, 1852.

III. EUGENIA A., b. March 15, 1855.

IV. GEORGE M., b. August 29, 1857.

V.   HIBBARD E., b. June 20, 1861.   d. March 3, 1864.

VI. LIZZIE O., b. May 11, 1864.

No. 263.

WILLIAM SAYRE CARY, son of Daniel, No. 140, b. at Drakesville, N. J., 1822; m. Phebe Northup, 1852, and resides on the homestead farm.

His children were:

I.   ANN ELIZA, b. 1853.

II. SIMON N., b. 1855.

III. LEWIS, b. 1857.

No. 264.

JOHN CARY, son of Zenas, No. 142, b. in Colerain, Mass., July 24, 1810; m. first, Olive Watson, February 27, 1835, she d. October 2, 1852; and he m. second, Catherine Coolidge, September 22, 1853; she d. October 23, 1864; third, Lizzie J. White, January 23, 1867. He was living in Leyden, Mass., 1867.

His children were:

I.   EMERSON J.,* b. May 3, 1837.

II.   MARY S., b. January 12, 1840.   d. January 4, 1851.

III. FANNY O., b. June 18, 1842.

IV.   LYDIA A., b. August 25, 1844.

V.   JAMES P., b. May 18, 1848.

VI.   EVA E., b. January 21, 1855.

VII. ELLEN B., b. August 25, 1858.

*EMERSON J., m. Lydia D. Davenport, August 29, 1858; resides in North Adams, Mass.; has daughter, Lela, b. May 7, 1865.

No. 265.

GEORGE CARY, son of Zenas, No. 142, b. in Colerain,
Mass., July 4, 1812; m. first, Diara Shipper, January 7,1837,
she d. September 21, 1854; and he m. second, Dordana
Shipger, November 1, 1855; was living in Colerain, 1867.

His children were:

    I. CLARK S., b. October 3, 1838.   m. Minnie L.
            Goodel, April 18. 1867.
   II. ELLA D., b. October 5, 1856. d. April 22,1859.

No. 266.

WILLIAM W. CARY, son of Zenas, No. 142, b. in Colerain, Mass., February 24, 1815; m. first, Brittania W. Maxam, July 5. 1838, she d. August 9, 1842; and he m. second,
Harriet M. Maxam, May 21, 1843; and was residing in
Colerain, 1867.

His children were:

I. SARAH E., b. June 12, 1840. d. September 8, 1842.

II. WILLIAM H., b. July 19, 1842. d. September 1842.

III. WILLIAM H., b. December 18, 1846. d. September 15, 1847

IV. WILLIAM W., b. November 6, 1848.

V. SARAH F., b. July 13, 1850.

VI. VIOLA E., b. September 22, 1853.

VII. CHARLES T., b. May 16, 1857. d. August 15, 1857.

No. 267.

LEVI CARY, son of Zenas, No. 142, b. in Colerain, Mass., April 2, 1822; m. Fanny J. Shipper, November 27, 1845, and resided in Ashfield, Mass., in 1867.

His children were:

   I.   HOYT FRANCIS, b. October 11, 1847.

   II. ARTHUR D., b. March 1, 1853. d. August 31, 1857.

  III. EMMA L., b. October 1, 1855. d. August 28, 1857.

  IV. NELLIE G., b. May 16, 1860.

   V. FRED. E., b. June 9, 1864.

No. 268.

JOSIAH CARY, son of Zebulon, No. 143, b. at Brookfield, Mass., September 25, 1814; was a carpenter by trade; removed to and resided in Franklinville, Chatauque county, N. Y. He d. September 29, 1865; he m. Anne Butler, 1843.

His children were:

   I.   PHEBE ANN, b. January 2, 1844.

   II. WILLIAM H., b. January 2, 1846.

  III. SUSAN, b. May 7, 1849.

No. 269.

Josiah Addison Cary, son of Josiah, No. 144, b. in Brookfield, Mass., 1813; removed to Ohio; was superintendent of Deaf and Dumb Asylum, at Columbus, where he d. August 7, 1852. He m. Gertrude Jenkins, October 23, 1844, she is still living and conducting a popular young ladies seminary, at Philadelphia, Pa.

His children were:

    I. Mary Alice, b. May 5, 1846.

    II. Norman White, b. October 29, 1849.

No. 270.

Nathan C. Cary, son of Avery, No. 145, b. in North Brookfield, Mass., 1814; m. Frances T. Wilson, 1855, and resides in Roxbury, Mass.

His children were:

    I. Fanny M., b. 1846.

    II. William A., b. 1849.

    III. Mary E., b. 1854. d. 1855.

No. 271.

Samuel A. Cary, son of Avery, No. 145, b. in North
Brookfield, Mass., 1823 ; m. Maria Cook, in Boston, Mass.,
1853, and settled in Elyria, Ohio.

His children were;

 I. Edvard A., b. 1856.

 II. Harriet, b. 1858.

 III. Annie, ⎫

        ⎬ b. and d. 1861.

 IV. Mary. ⎭

No. 272.

Daniel Moulton Cary, son of Thomas H., No. 147,
b. in Springville, N. Y., June 25, 1831 ; m. Celestine Gates,
March, 1856 ; resides at Allen's Point, Wisconsin.

His children were:

 I. Edvard, b. 1857.

 II. Beniamin, b. 1860.

No. 273.

CHARLES CARY, son of Caleb, No. 150, b. in East Machias, Me., 1835; m. Mary E., daughter of Luther Cary, 1857, and resides in East Machias.

His children were :

   I. WILLIAM, b. 1858.

  II. LUCY T., b. 1860.

No. 274.

ELISHA CALEB CARY, son of Jonathan, No. 151, b. in Cooper, Me., 1819; m. Vienna Bridgman, 1846; resides in Cooper.

His children were;

    I. LAURA E.,

   II. VERANUS L.

  III. ALVIN S.

  IV. MANLY A.

   V. FRANK E.

  VI. ELISHA S.

No. 275.

HENRY S. CARY, son of Jonathan, No. 151, b. in Cooper, Me., 1821; m. Waity Palmeter, 1845; resides in Cooper.

His children were:

    I.   ELIZABETH M.

    II. EUNICE E.

    III. PRISCILLA C.

No. 276.

JAMES WEBBER CARY, son of Luther, No. 152, b. in East Machias, Me., August, 1819; m. Anna E. Allan, October 1857; resides in Cooper, Me.

His children were:

    I. AMELIA, b. October, 1858.

    II. JOHN ALLAN, b. March, 1861.

No. 277.

CHARLES GEORGE CARY, son of Lewis, No. 155, b. in Boston, Mass., 1824; m. Sarah O. Barnes, 1848, and was accidentaly shot while hunting, 1853.

His children were;
I. GEORGE BILLINGS, b. 1849.
II. FRANCIS HENRY, b. 1851.
III. CHARLES WARREN, b. 1854.

No. 278.

THOMAS WEBB CARY, son of Lewis, No. 155, b. in Boston, Mass., 1826; m. Caroline Parker, 1846.

His children were:
I. CHARLES PARKER, b. 1847.
II. EMMA C., b. 1849.
III. LEWIS WARREN, b. 1851. d. 1856.
IV. ADELINE E., b. 1853.
V. MARY E., b. 1856.
VI. CALVIN CHASE, b. 1858.

No. 279.

ALEXANDER CLAXTON CARY, son of Isaac, No. 156, b. in Boston, Mass., February, 1834; m. Miss Barker, and resides in Boston.

His children were:

    I. LILLIAN.

    II. ALICE.

    III. ELIZABETH.

No. 280.

COL. SAMUEL CARY, son of Abram, No. 159, b. in New Jersey, 1784; removed with his parents to Northwest Territory, when a boy; m. Sarah Goble, in Cincinnati, October 25, 1803, and settled in Henry county, Ind.; he was a man of quiet and amiable temper, a nobleman by nature; was a great favorite with the Indians; an early and prominent freemason; he came to his death by accident, August 27, 1828; his wife a model woman, d. at the age of 71 years.

His children were:

I. .RHODA,* b. January 25, 1805.

II. MARY M.,† b. May, 1807.

III. DRUSILLA,‡ b. February 3. 1809.

IV. LEONORA, b. November 12, 1810. d. November 5, 1814.

V. MARTHA,‖ ⎫
⎬ b. October 6, 1812.
VI. EBENEZER,§ ⎭

VII. SAMUEL STEPHEN DECATUR, (a) b. March 29, 1815.

VIII. SUSANNA, b. May 23, 1817. d. November 10, 1826.

*RHODA, m. A. W. Reid, of South Carolina, October 2, 1823; d. at Grand Gulph, La., in 1848, leaving four sons and two daughters,

†MARY M., m. Dr. John Elliott, October 25, 1826; has one son and two daughters.

†DRUSILLA, m. J. B. Ferguson, of Indianapolis, Ind.; December 18, 1823; d. 1853, leaving three sons and one daughter.

‖MARTHA, m. Lorenzo D. Meeks, of New Castle, Ind., September 23, 1831; has four sons and three daughters.

§EBENEZER, was a Captain in the Mexican War, and d. in the city of Mexico, in 1848; he m. Mary Elsrath, 1837, and d. childless.

(a)SAMUEL S, D., m. Mary D. Owens, July 22, 1833, in New Castle, Ind.; had three sons and two daughters; went to Mexican War; d, in Puebla, Mexico, 1848; his widow went south; his two sons, Fielding G., and Martin, were in the Confederate army, and I have no further trace of them. Both daughters d. childless.

IX.　Oliver H. Perry,(*b*)　b. February 26, 1819.

X.　Sarah A. M.,(*c*)　b. February 6, 1822.

XI.　James Noble,(*d*)　b. June 18, 1823.

XII.　John Test,(*e*)　b. 1825.

No. 281.

Waitsell Munson Cary, son of Abram, No. 159, b·
in New Jersey; removed with parents to Cincinnati, thence
to Springfield, Ohio, where he m. Nancy Rock, July 9, 1805;
removed to Knightstown, Indiana, among the first settlers,
where he lived to an advanced age, highly esteemed.

(*b*)Oliver H, P., was a Captain in the Mexican war; was a Lieuten-
ant-Colonel of the 36th Indiana Regiment, in the late war.　m. Lois Hall,
resides at Marion, Grant county, Ind.; had one daughter, living.

(*c*)Sarah, m. Bronson Swaim, September 22, 1847; lives at Knightstown, Ind.; has two sons and one daughter.

(*d*)James N., served in the army during the Mexican war, and d. soon
after returning home.

(*e*)John T., served in the army during the Mexican war; went to California in 1850; was distinguished as a lawyer, and for the past fifteen years
has been on the bench in Klamath county, Cal.; unm.

His children were:

I. ABRAM,* b. November 11, 1807.

II. MARTHA,† b. January 20, 1809.

III. MARY,‡ b. November 7, 1810.

IV. ELEANOR,‖ b. September 11, 1812.

V. PHEBE,§ b. April 4, 1814.

VI. ROSANNA,(*a*) b. March 5, 1816.

VII. CAROLINE,(*b*) b. 1818.

No. 282.

HENRY AXTELL CARY, son of Nathaniel, No. 162, b. in New Jersey, November 4, 1816; was a tanner by trade; m. Mary Bockover, 1839; lives in Towanda, Pa.

*ABRAM, m. Elizabeth Sprause, and had: I. Nancy E., b. September 1, 1849. II. Waitsell M., b. February 18, 1851. III. Henrietta, b. January, 1853. IV. Joseph M., b. October, 1854. V. Mary H., b. November, 1856. VI. Rosa E., b. January, 1862.

†MARTHA, m. first, Benjamin Stratton, January 26, 1832; second, Jesse Hinshaw; had three sons and two daughters.

‡MARY, m. Asa Heaton, February 4, 1830; had three sons, viz.: Abram C., Joseph W., and Waitsell M.

‖ELEANOR, m. J. M. Whitesill, August 18, 1831; had two sons, viz.: James Lowry and Charles Rock.

§PHEBE, m. Robert Hudleson, June 10, 1830; had four sons and two daughters.

(*a*)ROSANNA, m. M. F. Edwards, May 5, 1836; and had two sons and three daughters.

(*b*)CAROLINE, m. D. Macy, 1834; d. childless, 1836.

His children were :

I.   JEFFERSON S., b. October, 1840. In U. S. Navy.

II.   FRANK B., b. April, 1842.   Killed at the battle
        of Chancellorsville, 1862.

III.   ANN AUGUSTA, b. June, 1848.

No. 283,

LEVIS CARY, son of Lewis, No. 162, b. in New Jersey,
June 13, 1820 ; m. Julia A. Ensign, August 31, 1845 ; is an
extensive manufacturer of coach lamps, in Newark, N. J.

His children were ;

I.   AMELIA, b. July 7, 1846.

II.   WILLIAM H., b. July 2, 1848.

III.   JOHN C., b. January 19, 1851.

IV.   EDVARD P., b. June 23, 1853.   d. January 13,
        1854.

V.   ALFRED E., b. October 23, 1855.   d. November
        14, 1861

VI.   EMMA M., b. October 5. 1862.

No. 284.

Isaac Cary, son of Nathaniel, No. 162, b. in New Jersey, March 22, 1823; m. Harriet Rowe, August 31, 1854; is a physician, and resides in Norwich, Orange county, N. J.

His children were:

I.   Frank R., b. 1856.

No. 285.

William Henry Cary, son of William, No. 167, b. in Graniteville, R. I., May 17, 1837; a stonecutter by occupation; m. Claretta A. Davis, in Pawtucket, R. I., January 13, 1861.

His children were:

I.   Frederick A., ⎫
II. Franklin E., ⎬ b. Dec. 29, 1865. d. Mar. 10, 1866.

III. Henry, ⎫
IV. Elma, ⎬ b. April 18, 1868. d. April 29, 1868.

No. 286.

George W. Cary, son of George S., No. 168, b. in Phenix Village, R. I., June 11, 1829 ; a boot and shoe dealer ; m. Martha W. Hill, June 28, 1849, and lives in New Haven, Ct.

His children were ;

  I. Edna Dora, b. January 5. 1850. d. February 18, 1857.
  II. George S., b. May 6, 1852. Living in New Haven, Connecticut.

No. 287.

William H. Cary, son of George S., No. 168, b. in Lippit, R. I., August 31, 1831 ; a farmer ; m. Nellie N. Converse, May 19, 1862, and resides in Worcester, Mass.

His children were :

  I. William Pliny, b. January 7, 1865.

No. 288.

Edvard M. Cary, son of George S., No. 168, b. in Thompson, Ct., April 28, 1834 ; a manufacturer ; m. Ester J. Benham, September 24, 1863, and resides in Detroit, Mich.

His children were :

  I. Edvard Lincoln, b. March 8, 1865.

No. 289.

CALVIN CARY, son of Richard M., No. 173, b. in Boston, Erie county, N. Y., October 1, 1816; m. Orilla S. Drake, November 30, 1837; removed to Johnstown, Rock county, Wisconsin, where he d. November 26, 1858; she d. August 21, 1868.

His children were :

    I. ROLLIN, b. October 16, 1838.   d. December 25, 1838.

    II. ARAMITTA, b. August 25, 1843.   d. September 28, 1843.

    III. LELAND J., b. September 27, 1846.   d. November 3, 1863.

No. 290.

EPHRAIM CARY, son of Richard M., No. 173, b. in Boston, Erie county, N. Y., October 27, 1818; m. Emily Shumway, in Johnstown, Wisconsin, April 22, 1846, where he still resides.

His children were :

    I. ORINDA, b. August 14, 1847.

    II. EUGENE L., b. November 16, 1849.

    III. ANNE G., b. November 13, 1851

    IV. EMMA, b. May 28, 1856.

No. 291

BENJAMIN T. CARY, son of Richard M., No. 173, b. in
Boston, Erie county, New York, February 15, 1821; m.
Sarah M. Skinner, March 20, 1845, and resides in Janesville,
Wisconsin.   She d. June 17, 1874.

His children were :

   I.   LEVI F., b. July 16, 1846.   d. October 14, 1846.

   II. ARTHUR W., b. October 30, 1847.   d. October
28, 1868.

  III. EMERY, b. September 7, 1849.   d. February 29,
1852.

  IV. EDDIE, b. May 10, 1853.

   V. ELMER E., b. December 29, 1855.

  VI. LILLIAN M., b. January 30, 1858.

No. 292.

RICHARD CARY, son of Richard M., No. 173, b. in Boston, Erie county, N. Y., April 8, 1830; m. Julia Osborn,
January 1, 1853; resides at Johnstown, Wisconsin.

His children were;

   I.——— a son, b. August 31, 1856.   d. September
30, 1856.

   II. EMERY C., b. March 12, 1860.

No. 293.

MELVIN CARY, son of Richard M., No. 173, b. in Boston, Erie county, N. Y., June 28, 1834; m. Helen Thayer, October 4, 1851; resides in Johnstown, Wisconsin.

His children were:

    I.   DELIA L., b. April 18, 1860.

    II.   EDITH M., b. March 16, 1862.

    III.   IDA M., b. May 19, 1864.

No. 294.

SYLVESTER L. CARY, son of Van Rensalaer, No. 178, b. February 23, 1827; m. Clara J. Daniels, 1855; resides at Glen Roy, Iowa; a merchant.

His children were:

    I.   ALICE S., b. April 16, 1856.

    II.   HOVARD L., b. April 21, 1860.

    III.   JAMES V., b. January 16, 1862.

    IV.   EDDIE S., b. June 28, 1864.

    V.   CLINTON C., b. September 28, 1867,

No. 295.

John W. Cary, son of Van Rensalaer, No. 178, b. March 5, 1829; m. Harriet E. Midbery, July, 1849; resides at Medoc, Jasper county, Illinois; belonged to 74th Illinois regiment, in the Union Army.

His children were:

I.　Sophronia, b. 1851.
II.　Clara, b. 1856.
III.　Ines, b. 1858.
IV.　Emory, b. 1860.

No. 296.

Alfred William Cary, son of Elijah, No. 184, b. in Scotland, Ct., July 24, 1819; m. Sarah E. Cross, March 27, 1844; is a mechanic and farmer; resides on the farm of his great grand-father, John Cary, No. 49, which has been retained in the family.

His children were;

I.　Sarah L., b. July 19, 1846.
II.　Charles A., b. May 3, 1860.

No. 297.

HENRY LORIN CARY, son of Elijah, No. 184, b. in Scotland, Ct., November 21, 1824; m. first, Martha R. Gris-wold, January 13, 1848, moved to Petersburg, Va., where his wife d. November 17, 1855; he m. second, Eliza Whitting-: ton, July 7, 1859, and removed to St. Paul, Minnesota, where. he resides.

His children were:

I. MARTHA V., b. November 12, 1855.   d. December 11, 1855.

II. GEORGE HENRY, b. March 23, 1860.   d. May 7, 1860.

III. WILLIAM HENRY, b. January 19, 1861.

IV. GEORGIANA E., b. July 31, 1864.

No. 298,

THERON CARY, son of William, No. 185, b. in Scotland, Ct., December 16, 1810; m. Hannah Bishop, July 8, 1844; resides in Middletown, Ct.

His children were:

I. HARRIET B., b. February 16, 1848.   d. July 11, 1853.

II. EDWIN W., b. July 27, 1849.

No. 299.

FREDERICK WILLIAM CARY, son of William, No. 185, b. in Scotland, Ct., June 6, 1813; m. first, Henrietta R. Woodworth, February 1, 1837, she d. July 9, 1852; he m. second, Rachel Woodworth, October 11, 1853, and resides in Greenville, Ct.

His children were:

I.   MARY L., b. November 28, 1838.

II. ELLEN M., b. January 6, 1841. d. February 26, 1849.

III. CHARLES W., b. July 15, 1843.

IV. ANDREV E., b. December 11, 1845.

V.   FRANCES W., b. February 23, 1852. d. September 22, 1852.

VI. FREDERICK, b. December 9, 1854. d. March 8, 1855.

VII. WALTER L., b. May 15, 1857. d. November 20, 1857.

No. 300.

HORACE CARY, son of William, No. 185, b. in Scotland, Ct., August 15, 1819; m. Cornelia E. Brown, June 14, 1847; removed to and resides at Berlin, Ills.

His children were:

I.   WILLIAM H., b. November 2, 1848.

II.   HERBERT O., b. March 6, 1850.

III.   EDGAR A,, b. December 29, 1851.

IV.   FREDERICK A., b. March 28, 1853.

V.   CHARLES H., b. April 12, 1855. d. March 12,

VI.   OSCAR E., b. December 27, 1856.

VII.   FRANK L., b. December 10, 1859.

VIII.   ALICE A., b. July 20, 1861.

No. 301.

WILLIAM L. CARY, son of Frederick, No. 186, b. in Knox county, Ohio, September 22, 1822; m. Eveline Graham, October 29, 1851; is a farmer and resides in Knox county, Ohio

His children were:

I.   RALPH W., b. July 2, 1852.

II.   HENRY Y., b. January 4, 1854.

III.   SAMUEL F., b. October 11, 1855.

IV.   JOHN W·, b. October 9, 1858.

V.   EVALINE E., b. August 24, 1860.

VI.   WILLIAM, b. November 1862.

No. 302.

WINTHROP H. CARY, son of Ralph, No. 187, b. in Hartord, Ct., 1818 ; m. Sarah Hills, 1840 ; resides in Hartford, Ct.

His children were;

   I.   ELLEN A., b. 1842.

   II. EMILY L., b. 1844.

No. 303.

. JAMES S. CARY, son of Ralph. No. 187, b. in Hartford, Ct., 1820 ; m. Betsy Ann Alger, 1847.

 His children were:

   I.   LUCIEN B. b. 1848.   Removed to Mississippi, and have no further records.

No. 304,

GEORGE H. CARY, son of Ralph, No. 187, b. in Hartford, Ct., 1823 ; m. Annie A. Haven ; resides in Hartford.

His children were:

   I.   GEORGE H., b. 1852.

   II. FRANK S., b. 1854.

No. 305.

JAMES BENEIJAH CARY, son of James, No. 188, b. in Canterbury, Ct., August 22, 1810; is a farmer residing in Connecticut ; m. Mary B. Adams.

His children were :

I.   ASA B.,* b. 1835.

II. FITCH A., b. 1838.   Merchant.   unm.

III. ELIZABETH, b. 1840.   unm.

IV. GEORGE L., b. 1842.   Co. A, 1st Connecticut Cavalry.

V.   DWIGHT,† b. 1846.

No. 306.

HENRY HUDSON CARY, son of Sanford, No. 189, b. in Scotland, Ct., July 2, 1814; a farmer in Scotland ; m. Persis Geer, 1840.

His children were:

I. CAROLINE TRACY, b. 1845.

II. ELIZA JANE, b. 1849.

*ASA B., graduated at West Point, 1858; was ordered to Utah, distinguished himself at the battle of " Apache Canon ;" was promoted to a Captaincy in U. S. A., and in 1863 was in command at Fort Union, New Mexico.

†DWIGHT, was in Co. F, 8th Connecticut Regiment, and was killed at the battle of Antietam, September 17, 1862.

No. 307.

DVIGHT CARY, son of Sanford, No. 189, b. in Scotland, Ct., February 24, 1817 ; a farmer in Scotland ; m. Susan Bass, 1843.

His children were :

    I.   SARAH ROSETTA, b. 1844.

    II. MARTHAETTE,
    III. MARYETTE, } b. 1846.   d. 1848.

    IV. ANN BRADFORD, b. 1848.

    V. FRANK WINSLOW, b. 1850.

    VI. SANFORD, b. 1853.   d. 1858.

    VII. JANE LUCRETIA. b. 1856.

  VIII. GEORGE SANFORD, b. 1860.

No. 308.

WALCOTT CARY, son of Sanford, No. 189, b. in Scotland, Ct., June 29, 1819, a farmer in Hampton, Ct.; m. Lucy Ann Burnham, of Windham, Ct., 1842.

His children were ;

    I.   MARY JOSEPHINE, b. 1843. m. Henry E. Holt, 1861.

    II. JULIAN, b. 1846.

    III. GEORGE CLINTON, b. 1848.

    IV. WILLIAM BURNHAM, b. 1856.

No. 309.

JONATHAN T. CARY, son of Josiah, No. 202, b. in Haddam, Ct., March 31, 1823; m. first, Rhuca Mead, March 7, 1844, she d. April, 1845; he m. second, Lucy C. Lear, March 10, 1849; resides in Schenectady county, N. Y.

His children were;

    I.   ——— a son, b April, 1845. d. May, 1845.

    II.· SUSAN M.

    III. GEORGE NEVTON.

    IV. RHUCA.

No. 310.

CLARK W. CARY, son of Josiah, No. 202, b. in Haddam, Ct., January 28, 1825; was an extensive leather merchant, in New York city, of the firm of Mulford & Cary; m. Mary E. Doyle, February 18, 1852. He d. March 7, 1871.

His children were:

    I. JOSIAH WILLARD, b. January 22, 1853.

    II. CLARK HENRY, b. October 19, 1854.

    III. MARY IDA b. December 2, 1856. d.

    IV. ALBERT FERRIS, b. February 27, 1859.

No. 311.

Jedediah T. Cary, son of Josiah, No. 202, b. in Haddam, Ct., February 13, 1833; m. Lucy Ann Bromley, April 12, 1857.

His children were;

   I. Charles,

   II. Albert.

   III. Sarah Jane,

No. 312.

Benjamin H. Cary, son of Josiah, No. 202, b. in Haddam, Ct., January 26, 1835; m. Phebe E. Komorinskey, May 13, 1858, and resides in New York city.

His children were :

   I. Alice Eliza, b. February 24, 1859.

   II. Edwin Augustus, b. July 27, 1863.

Explanations and Abbreviations,

It is almost impossible in a work of this kind to arrange the records so that each person can readily find his own name, and trace backward and forward his family history. After examining a great number of similar works, I have adopted an arrangement of my own.

I have arranged the records by generations, beginning with the common ancestor, John, as the first generation,— his children, the second ; grand children, the third and so on.

In all cases I have commenced the generation with the children of the eldest brother in each family and closed with the youngest.

Any person finding his or her name in the index will be referred to the page where the family record is found. The person will find the name of the immediate ancestor with the No. of his family record in the preceding generation, and so on, back to the common ancestor. The No. at the right of the name indicates the place where the descendants of the next generation will be found. The Roman numerals at the left of each name points out the order of birth, or the place in the particular family.

b.	Born.	d.	Died.
m.	Married.	unm.	Unmarried.
n. t.	No trace of descendants.		

The notes explain themselves, and when they occur indi-cate that no other mention is made of the person.

Where the same name is found in the index in the same generation, to aid in finding the one sought the birth place or residence is added.

We have added an index in alphabetical order of the names of persons with whom marriages have been had, for the convenience of those who would know their maternal an-cestor.

We hope that with these words of explanation any one may in a few minutes find their names and the connecting links backward and forward.

RELATIONSHIP.

If you wish to find your relationship to any other person in the volume, you will count backward to the common ancestor and then downward to the person whose relationship you seek, each generation, being termed in the law a degree—thus cousins are related in the fourth degree—the children of one cousin with the other cousin, are the fifth degree—the rela-tion of the children of cousins, is the sixth degree removed ; and are called cousins in the sixth degree.

INDEX.

FIND the name you seek and the figures denote where the name is first recorded, and then you can readily trace the ancestors or descendants. When the same christian name occurs more than once in the same generation, the place of birth or residence is added to aid in identifying the person sought. Even with this precaution you may have to look two or three times before you find the right person, as the same name occurs frequently having the same place of residence.

The names of persons with whom CARYS have intermarried are given in alphabetical order in generations, the figures denoting the page where the name is found. This will enable their descendants to trace their relation to the Cary Family.

First Generation.

Second Generation.

Third Generation

Fourth Generation.

Fifth Generation.

Sixth Generation.

Seventh Generation.

Eighth Generation.

Ninth Generation.

INDEX TO INTERMARRIAGES.

-•-•-•-

Fourth Generation.

Fifth Generation.

Eighth Generation.